MW01294350

This book is of a limited edition print.
Additional copies are available on request.

Please email:
info@browniesguidetoexpertlydefinedideas.com
for your specific needs.

Brownie's Guide To Expertly Defined Ideas

Volume 2

By

Verdes

This book is:

Friendly
Helpful
Straightforward
&
Slightly absurd

A dictionary for defining your ideas.

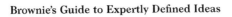

Brownie's Guide to Expertly Defined Ideas

verdes.nyc

All rights reserved.
Which includes the right to reproduce this book or portions thereof without asking first.

Second printing: March 2016. Printed in U.S.A.

We have no idea.

Let's admit that we don't really know where ideas come from.

There's no formula. No repeatable process. No surefire technique for success. Great ideas can happen to anyone at anytime. To a genius, a drunk or a drunk genius. And it's exactly this unpredictability that makes them so rare, delicate and precious. While every idea ends somewhere different, they all start in the same place – your head.

This book is a tool for taking the ideas inside your head and sharing them with all the people who live outside of it. Just like a dictionary defines words, these pages can be used to define your thoughts. Whether it's a new product, service, business, movie, book, website, music video, advertising campaign, version of yourself, or any other concept you'd like to realize, crystallizing your idea down to 4 - 6 words will let you express it clearly. These 4 - 6 words become guidelines, a set of parameters to help you decide what will help or hurt your idea and anticipate how it will behave in the future.

Whatever your ambition might be, we hope this book helps you accomplish it. New ideas are powerful tools for creating change, value and amusement. Lord knows the world could use more of all three.

How to use this book:

This book is a tool for defining your idea by reducing it down to between 4 - 6 essential words.

Try and use as few words as possible without missing any key characteristics, but don't let yourself go over 6 words. Remember, the best way to give your idea a chance to live is by making it simple and easy to understand.

Go from broad to specific. Drill down until the words are exact. As the words narrow, you will find yourself closer to clarity and ownability and further from cliche'. This book is designed to help you start wide and zero in on the essentials.

Having trouble starting? Think of your idea as a person. What qualities and characteristics do they have? How you you describe them to others?

Any idea that helps you define your idea is fair game. There is no formula to having a breakthrough, but hopefully these pages help you get your start.

My idea is:

My idea is:

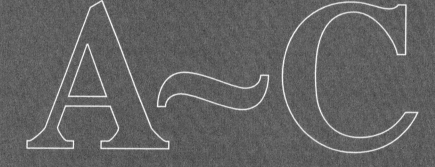

Accessible · Creative

Accessible

Accepting

It is the mark of an educated mind to be able to entertain a thought without accepting it.
— Aristotle

There is no place, no country, more compassionate more generous more accepting and more welcoming than the United States of America.
— Arnold Schwarzenegger

Agreeable

Animals are such agreeable friends - they ask no questions, they pass no criticisms.
— Mary Ann Evans

My idea of an agreeable person is a person who agrees with me.
— Benjamin Disraeli

Approachable

If you go out looking for friends, you're going to find they are very scarce. If you go out to be a friend, you'll find them everywhere.
— Zig Ziglar

I'd like to be more approachable not less weird.
— Chloe Sevigny

Avuncular

Uncle = Dad + Fun
— Craig Damrauer

You can tell your uncle stuff that you could not tell your dad.
— Dusty Baker

Be peaceful, be courteous, obey the
law, respect everyone; but if someone puts his hand on you, send him
to the cemetery.
— Malcolm X

Courteous treatment will make a
customer a walking advertisement.
— James Cash Penney

Courteous

The rule of friendship means
there should be mutual sympathy
between them, each supplying
what the other lacks and trying
to benefit the other, always using
friendly and sincere words.
— Marcus Tullius Cicero

Friendship is a pretty full-time
occupation if you really are
friendly with somebody.
— Truman Capote

Friendly

We are trying to construct a more
inclusive society. We are going to
make a country in which no one is
left out.
— Franklin D. Roosevelt

A Tribe Called Quest's music was so
inclusive, so conscious, it brought
such a community together.
— Michael Rapaport

Inclusive

To be totally understanding makes
one very indulgent.
— Madame de Stael

You should not be replacing more
than one meal a day with ice cream.
— Jerry Greenfield

Indulgent

Neighborly

I want you to be concerned about your next door neighbor. Do you know your next door neighbor?
— Mother Teresa

Your own safety is at stake when your neighbor's wall is ablaze.
— Horace

Nice

Always be nice to your children because they are the ones who will choose your rest home.
— Phyllis Diller

It is nice to be important, but it's more important to be nice.
— John Templeton

Open

There's just some magic in truth and honesty and openness.
— Frank Ocean

In whatever number of years I have on Earth, I think that promoting the values of free expression, the openness of the Internet, that's the best use of my time.
— Eric Schmidt

Pleasant

There are more pleasant things to do than beat up people.
— Muhammad Ali

Be pleasant until ten o'clock in the morning and the rest of the day will take care of itself.
— Elbert Hubbard

Public sentiment is everything. With
public sentiment, nothing can fail.
Without it, nothing can succeed.
— Abraham Lincoln

The public is the only critic whose
opinion is worth anything at all.
— Mark Twain

Public

It's extremely important to
have a loyal fan base and be
receptive to them.
— Mike McCready

When people are smiling they are
most receptive to almost anything
you want to teach them.
— Allen Funt

Receptive

Accessible - Creative

Amazing

Astonishing

I get to go to work and come home with something interesting or enriching or astonishing.
— Diane Sawyer

Software tends not to kill people, and so we accept incredibly fast innovation loops because the consequences are tolerable and the results are astonishing.
— Dan Kaminsky

Awesome

The moment one gives close attention to anything, even a blade of grass it becomes a mysterious, awesome, indescribably magnificent world in itself.
— Henry Miller

One thing about a skater: they never quit. So a skater, to sum it up, is awesome.
— Lil Wayne

Dazzling

Give me the splendid silent sun, with all his beams full-dazzling.
— Walt Whitman

The truth must dazzle gradually or every man be blind.
— Emily Dickinson

Electric

Enthusiasm is the electricity of life. How do you get it? You act enthusiastic until you make it a habit.
— Gordon Parks

I've always loved the electric guitar: to hold it and work it and hear what it does is unreal.
— David Lynch

A girl should be two things:
classy and fabulous.
— Coco Chanel

Nowadays you can go anywhere in
the world in a few hours, and nothing is fabulous any more.
— Roald Dahl

Fabulous

Stuff your eyes with wonder, live as
if you'd drop dead in ten seconds.
See the world. It's more fantastic
than any dream made or paid for
in factories.
— Ray Bradbury

No one is going to try to fill my
mother's shoes, what she did was
fantastic. It's about making your
own future and your own destiny
and Kate will do a very good job
of that.
— Prince William

Fantastic

There are only two kinds of people
who are really fascinating - people
who know absolutely everything,
and people who know absolutely
nothing.
— Oscar Wilde

I think what makes people fascinating is conflict, it's drama, it's the
human condition. Nobody wants to
watch perfection.
— Nicolas Cage

Fascinating

Accessible - Creative

Incredible

Somewhere, something incredible is waiting to be known.
— Carl Sagan

What the Beatles did was something incredible, it was more than what a band could do.
— Yoko Ono

Magnificent

The courage of life is often a less dramatic spectacle than the courage of a final moment; but it is no less a magnificent mixture of triumph and tragedy.
— John F. Kennedy

The most corrosive piece of technology that I've ever seen is called television - but then, again, television, at its best, is magnificent.
— Steve Jobs

Marvelous

It is always the simple that produces the marvelous.
— Amelia Barr

I had my first French meal and I never got over it. It was just marvelous.
— Julia Child

Miraculous

Moralities, ethics, laws, customs, beliefs, doctrines - these are of trifling import. All that matters is that the miraculous become the norm.
— Henry Miller

The invariable mark of wisdom is to see the miraculous in the common.
— Ralph Waldo Emerson

Jazz music creates so many phenomenal figures.
— Wynton Marsalis

There are certain places in the
world that are kind of energy vor-
texes, which are phenomenal.
— Ian Somerhalder

Phenomenal

Once you replace negative
thoughts with positive ones, you'll
start having positive results.
— Willie Nelson

In order to carry a positive action
we must develop here a positive
vision.
— Dalai Lama

Positive
(see page 389)

(see page 389)

The most satisfying thing in life is
to have been able to give a large
part of one's self to others.
— Pierre Teilhard de Chardin

The pursuit of excellence is less
profitable than the pursuit of big-
ness, but it can be more satisfying.
— David Ogilvy

Satisfying

Accessible - Creative

People always say that my work is
sensational or shocking but there
are truly shocking things you could
do, and my sculptures don't go anywhere near that.
— Damien Hirst

I never travel without my diary.
One should always have something
sensational to read in the train.
— Oscar Wilde

Sensational

Spectacular

The view of Earth is spectacular.
— Sally Ride

My life hasn't always been a disaster, it's just that when it has, it's been a spectacular disaster.
— Boy George

Splendid

Nothing splendid was ever created in cold blood.
— Arnold H. Glasow

I like to be surrounded by splendid things.
— Freddie Mercury

Surprising

The secret to humor is surprise.
— Aristotle

A true leader always keeps an element of surprise up his sleeve, which others cannot grasp but which keeps his public excited and breathless.
— Charles de Gaulle

Terrific

Mike Tyson was one of the most terrific athletes I've ever met.
— Don King

President Reagan's one-liners were terrific.
— Geraldine Ferraro

An unexciting truth may be
eclipsed by a thrilling lie.
— Aldous Huxley

I get that same queasy, nervous,
thrilling feeling every time I go
to work.
— Steven Spielberg

Thrilling

Faith means believing the unbelievable.
— Gilbert K. Chesterton

Nothing is so unbelievable that
oratory cannot make it acceptable.
— Marcus Tullius Cicero

Unbelievable

Do something wonderful, people
may imitate it.
— Albert Schweitzer

Being the richest man in the cemetery doesn't matter to me. Going
to bed at night saying we've done
something wonderful, that's what
matters to me.
— Steve Jobs

Wonderful

Accessible - Creative

Authentic

Bona fide

I'm passionate about everything, like my family and friends. Anybody I am talkin' to is gonna be bona fide real. There is no substitution for happiness. Period.
— Suge Knight

Don't learn to do, but learn in doing. Let your falls not be on a prepared ground, but let them be bona fide falls in the rough and tumble of the world.
— Samuel Butler

Dependable

Without dependability one's ability may be a liability instead of an asset.
— Woodrow Wilson

Dependability is that quality of sureness which makes folks know that the task assigned will be accomplished, that the promise made will be kept, a golden quality.
— Clarissa A. Beesley

Faithful

Only the person who has faith in himself is able to be faithful to others.
— Erich Fromm

I haven't been faithful to my own advice in the past. I will in the future.
— Billy Graham

Genuine

Genuine poetry can communicate before it is understood.
— T. S. Eliot

A genuine man goes to the roots. To be a radical is no more than that: to go to the roots.
— Jose Marti

Being entirely honest with oneself
is a good exercise.
— Sigmund Freud

Tricks and treachery are the practice of fools, that don't have brains
enough to be honest.
— Benjamin Franklin

Honest
(see page 267)

Every man is a creative cause of
what happens, a primum mobile
with an original movement.
— Friedrich Nietzsche

Every great architect is - necessarily
- a great poet. He must be a great
original interpreter of his time, his
day, his age.
— Frank Lloyd Wright

Original

Character is like a tree and reputation like a shadow. The shadow is
what we think of it; the tree is the
real thing.
— Abraham Lincoln

Reality is wrong. Dreams are for real.
— Tupac Shakur

Real

What should young people do with
their lives today? Many things, obviously. But the most daring thing
is to create stable communities in
which the terrible disease of loneli-
ness can be cured.
— Kurt Vonnegut

There is nothing so stable as
change.
— Bob Dylan

Stable
(see page 441)

Accessible - Creative

True

Hard times arouse an instinctive desire for authenticity.
— Coco Chanel

There are only two mistakes one can make along the road to truth; not going all the way, and not starting.
— Buddha

Trusted

Whoever is careless with the truth in small matters cannot be trusted with important matters.
— Albert Einstein

To be trusted is a greater compliment than being loved.
— George MacDonald

Trustworthy

In a time of universal deceit - telling the truth is a revolutionary act.
— George Orwell

The United States established itself as a trustworthy new nation in its first two decades after the Revolutionary War by paying its debts, even when many in the country believed it had no obligation to do so.
— John Podhoretz

Balanced

Even

Treat all men alike. Give them the same law. Give them an even chance to live and grow.
— Chief Joseph

Respond intelligently even to unintelligent treatment.
— Lao Tzu

Grounded

Nothing profits more than self-esteem, grounded on what is just and right.
— John Milton

I walk slowly, but I never walk backwards.
— Abraham Lincoln

Harmonious

Imagine what a harmonious world it could be if every single person, both young and old shared a little of what he is good at doing.
— Quincy Jones

A formally harmonious product needs no decoration; it should be elevated through pure form.
— Ferdinand Porsche

Holistic

Every little action creates an effect: We are all interconnected.
— Yehuda Berg

I keep fit, I work out, I eat pretty damn well, I don't drink like a fish, and all of those things are tempered with a holistic mindset that you need to damn well respect the vehicle that you're walking around in.
— Mick Fleetwood

Never be in a hurry; do everything
quietly and in a calm spirit. Do not
lose your inner peace for anything
whatsoever, even if your whole
world seems upset.
— Saint Francis de Sales

Success is steady progress toward
one's personal goals.
— Jim Rohn

Level

The purpose of meditation is personal transformation.
— Henepola Gunaratana

Self-awareness is not just relaxation
and not just meditation. It must
combine relaxation with activity and
dynamism. Technology can aid that.
— Deepak Chopra

Meditative

Peace is not absence of conflict, it
is the ability to handle conflict by
peaceful means.
— Ronald Reagan

A peaceful man does more good
than a learned one.
— Pope John XXIII

Peaceful

The secret of happiness is to find a
congenial monotony.
— V. S. Pritchett

Set your life on fire. Seek those who
fan your flames.
— Rumi

Simpatico

Accessible - Creative

Stable
(see page 441)

Be sure you put your feet in the right place, then stand firm.
— Abraham Lincoln

The firm, the enduring, the simple, and the modest are near to virtue.
— Confucius

Beautiful

Alluring

Therefore, behold, I will allure her,
and bring her into the wilderness,
and speak comfortably unto her.
— The Bible

I find all that slightly destructive
but mad love alluring.
— Sienna Miller

Angelic

To love for the sake of being loved
is human, but to love for the sake of
loving is angelic.
— Alphonse de Lamartine

I saw the angel in the marble and
carved until I set him free.
— Michelangelo

Breath-taking

Life is not measured by the
breaths you take, but by its breathtaking moments.
— Michael Vance

And then, as he met my awed gaze,
he broke into a breathtaking smile
of exultation.
— Bella Swan

Cute

Cute is when your personality
shines through your looks.
— Natalie Portman

If I'm going to be 'too' anything,
'too cute' is fine. I love puppies. So
what? Who hates puppies?
— Zooey Deschanel

Look deep into nature, and then you
will understand everything better.
— Albert Einstein

With an eye made quiet by the
power of harmony, and the deep
power of joy, we see into the life
of things.
— William Wordsworth

Deep

But I think beautiful is simple
and elegant, like a ballad with
simple harmony.
— John Fogerty

It is not possible for a man to be
elegant without a touch of feminin-
ity.
— Vivienne Westwood

Elegant
(see page 155)

(see page 155)

It is not only fine feathers that
make fine birds.
— Aesop

All fine architectural values are
human values, else not valuable.
— Frank Lloyd Wright

Fine

Love is the flower you've got to
let grow.
— John Lennon

The flower that smells the sweetest
is shy and lowly.
— William Wordsworth

Floral

Even socialist dictators have an
interest in gorgeous supermodels.
— Hugo Chavez

Gorgeous hair is the best revenge.
— Ivana Trump

Gorgeous

Accessible - Creative

Graceful

Everyone is like a butterfly, they
start out ugly and awkward and
then morph into beautiful graceful
butterflies that everyone loves.
— Drew Barrymore

Like a graceful vase, a cat, even
when motionless, seems to flow.
— George F. Will

Faithful

I require three things in a man.
He must be handsome, ruthless
and stupid.
— Dorothy Parker

Being handsome wasn't much of a
burden. It worked for me.
— David Bailey

Lyrical

When I was growing up, Dr. Seuss
was really my favorite. There was
something about the lyrical nature
and the simplicity of his work that
really hit me.
— Tim Burton

Fiction and poetry are my first
loves, but the really beautiful lyrical
essay can do so much that other
forms cannot.
— Chris Abani

My style icons would be people like
Brigitte Bardot and old Hollywood
actresses who always look so stun-
ning, cool and chic.
— Jessica Brown Findlay

And I'm slightly in love with
Scarlett Johansson: she's just stun-
ning. And she's bright, which is
incredibly sexy.
— Daniel Radcliffe

Stunning

Beauty is that which is simultaneously attractive and sublime.
— Karl Wilhelm Friedrich Schlegel

There's only a step from the sublime
to the ridiculous, but there's no
road leading from the ridiculous to
the sublime.
— Lion Feuchtwanger

Sublime

Keep your eyes on the stars, and
your feet on the ground.
— Theodore Roosevelt

The real voyage of discovery consists not in seeking new landscapes,
but in having new eyes.
— Marcel Proust

Wide-eyed

Big

Abundant

As for time, all men have it in abundance.
— George S. Clason

An abundance of options does not make you feel privileged and indulged; too many options make you feel like all of them are wrong, and that you are wrong if you choose any of them.
— Susan Orlean

Broad

I have a very broad demographic, from the 8-year-old who knows every word to 'Ice Ice Baby' and the college kid who grew up on 'Ninja Rap' to the soccer mom and grandparent.
— Vanilla Ice

In a broad systems sense, an organism's environment is indistinguishable from the organism itself.
— Kevin Kelly

Colossal

The essence of life is statistical improbability on a colossal scale.
— Richard Dawkins

Few people sufficiently appreciate the colossal task of feeding a world of billions of omnivores who demand meat with their potatoes.
— Jonathan Safran Foer

Epic

The ode lives upon the ideal, the epic upon the grandiose, the drama upon the real.
— Victor Hugo

They only live to get radical.
— Bodhi

Yes, America is gigantic, but a
gigantic mistake.
— Sigmund Freud

If I have seen further than others,
it is because I was standing on the
shoulders of giants
— Isaac Newton

Gigantic

An icon is a statue carved in wood.
It was shocking at first, when I got
that reference.
— Debbie Harry

And so we gaze obediently at what
we are told to gaze at, without
exactly asking why.
— Julian Barnes

Iconic

Having a broken heart makes you
realize the immense capability it
possesses to mend and heal itself
and to love far more intensely,with
every affixed piece of it that was
once broken
— Sanhita Baruah

The sea is everything. It covers
seven tenths of the terrestrial globe.
Its breath is pure and healthy. It is
an immense desert, where man is
never lonely, for he feels life stirring
on all sides.
— Jules Verne

Immense

Ain't no snake that big.
— Ice Cube

The artist must bow to the monster
of his own imagination.
— Richard Wright

Monster

Mountainous

What are men to rocks and mountains?
— Jane Austen

Those who travel to mountain-tops
are half in love with themselves, and
half in love with oblivion.
— Robert Macfarlane

Panoramic

It was a comfort to sit up and
contemplate the majestic panorama
of mountains and valleys spread
out below us and eat ham and hard
boiled eggs. Nothing helps scenery
like ham and eggs.
— Mark Twain

We can't just have mainstream
behavior on television in a free society, we have to make sure we see the
whole panorama of human behavior.
— Jerry Springer

Substantial

Beware lest you lose the substance
by grasping at the shadow.
— Aesop

One realized all sorts of things. The
value of an illusion, for instance,
and that the shadow can be more
important than the substance.
— Jean Rhys

Thundering

None shall pass.
— Gandalf

Thunder is good, thunder is impressive; but it is lightning that does
the work.
— Mark Twain

If you have an important point
to make, don't try to be subtle or
clever. Use a pile driver. Hit the
point once. Then come back and
hit it again. Then hit it a third
time - a tremendous whack.
— Winston Churchill

Nobody realizes that some people
expend tremendous energy merely
to be normal.
— Albert Camus

Tremendous

Technology has become as ubiqui-
tous as the air we breathe, so we are
no longer conscious of its presence.
— Godfrey Reggio

Our demons are our own limita-
tions, which shut us off from the
realization of the ubiquity of the
spirit [...] each of these demons is
conquered in a vision quest.
— Joseph Campbell

Ubiquitous

The man who writes about himself
and his own time is the only man
who writes about all people and
all time.
— George Bernard Shaw

If your shout is local, only your vil-
lage will hear you; if your whisper
is universal, the whole world will
hear you!
— Mehmet Murat ildan

Universal

Vast

Dawn is an amazing thing. This same event had been occurring hundreds of millions - hundreds of billions - of times, from an age long before there had been anything resembling life on earth.
— Haruki Murakami

'I'm bored' is a useless thing to say. You live in a great, big, vast world that you've seen none percent of.
— Louis C. K.

Capable

Able

My most brilliant achievement was my ability to be able to persuade my wife to marry me.
— Winston Churchill

Entrepreneurs are simply those who understand that there is little difference between obstacle and opportunity and are able to turn both to their advantage.
— Niccolo Machiavelli

Adept

The young are adept at learning, but even more adept at avoiding it.
— P. J. O'Rourke

In the last few thousand years, we've become incredibly adept technically. We've treasured the controlling part of ourselves and neglected the surrendering part.
— Brian Eno

Advanced

Any sufficiently advanced technology is indistinguishable from magic.
— Arthur C. Clarke

We are just an advanced breed of monkeys on a minor planet of a very average star. But we can understand the Universe. That makes us something very special.
— Stephen Hawking

Apt

Perfection has one grave defect: it is apt to be dull.
— W. Somerset Maugham

An apt quotation is like a lamp which flings its light over the whole sentence.
— Letitia Elizabeth Landon

The works must be conceived with
fire in the soul but executed with
clinical coolness.
— Joan Miro

Clinical

There's a difference between
describing and evoking something.
You can describe something and be
quite clinical about it. To evoke it,
you call it up in the reader.
— Margaret Atwood

Just never forget to be dexterous
and deft. And never mix up your
right foot and your left. And will
you succeed? Yes! You will, indeed!
(98 and ¾ percent guaranteed.)
— Dr. Seuss

Deft

Any intelligent fool can make
things bigger, more complex, and
more violent. It takes a touch of
genius -- and a lot of courage -- to
move in the opposite direction.
— E. F. Schumacher

If you have to say or do something
controversial, aim so that people
will hate that they love it and not
love that they hate it.
— Criss Jami

Effective

Effective communication is 20%
what you know and 80% how you
feel about what you know.
— Jim Rohn

Efficient

Progress isn't made by early risers. It's made by lazy men trying to find easier ways to do something.
— Robert A. Heinlein

Just in terms of allocation of time resources, religion is not very efficient. There's a lot more I could be doing on a Sunday morning.
— Bill Gates

Effortless

Our ability to perceive the world around us seems so effortless that we tend to take it for granted.
— Vilayanur S. Ramachandran

21st century capitalism; easy indulgence and effortless self-love all available at a flick of the credit card.
— Geoff Mulgan

Handy

Once you get past funny, my other qualities are so below average. It's not like I'm handy.
— Seth Meyers

When ideas fail, words come in very handy.
— Johann Wolfgang von Goethe

Masterly

Part of the happiness of life consists not in fighting battles, but in avoiding them. A masterly retreat is in itself a victory.
— Norman Vincent Peale

Mastery is great, but even that is not enough. You have to be able to change course without a bead of sweat, or remorse.
— Tom Peters

If I've got food and water, as long as
I can exercise my mind and keep it
nimble, then I'll be okay.
— Rob Walton

When you get lost in your imagina-
tory vagueness your foresight will
become a nimble vagrant.
— Gary Busey

Nimble

There's something about having
a badge that just makes you feel
so official.
— Gloria Reuben

The message here is you cannot,
under any circumstances, throw
an object at an official. You just
cannot do it.
— Stu Jackson

Official

I would like to see anyone, prophet,
king or God, convince a thousand
cats to do the same thing at the
same time.
— Neil Gaiman

Science is organized knowledge.
Wisdom is organized life.
— Immanuel Kant

Organized

You have to not listen to the nay
sayers because there will be many
and often they'll be much more
qualified than you and cause you
to sort of doubt yourself.
— James Cameron

You are just as qualified as any
expert to make a judgment and
have a feeling or a response to any
work of art.
— Bill Viola

Qualified

Accessible - Creative

Ready

I've heard there are troubles of more than one kind; some come from ahead, and some come from behind. But I've brought a big bat. I'm all ready, you see; now my troubles are going to have troubles with me!
— Dr. Seuss

The man who goes alone can start today; but he who travels with another must wait till that other is ready.
— Henry David Thoreau

Skillful

The greater the difficulty the more glory in surmounting it. Skillful pilots gain their reputation from storms and tempests.
— Epictetus

Lionel Messi is a wonderful player. Very skillful. Highly intelligent. He is not good in the air.
— Pele

Useful

Being good is commendable, but only when it is combined with doing good is it useful
— Stephen King

A lighthouse is more useful than a church.
— Benjamin Franklin

Up to it

A man's gotta do what a man's gotta do.
— John Wayne

Your mission, should you choose to accept it...
— Mission Commander Swanbeck

Well-oiled

Oh the nerves, the nerves; the mysteries of this machine called man! Oh the little that unhinges it, poor creatures that we are!
— Charles Dickens

'Fast & Furious' is a well-oiled machine. Those guys really know what they're doing. The guys that work behind the scenes are just as important as the ones in front of the cameras.
— Laz Alonso

Accessible - Creative

Casual

Comfortable

Nothing consoles and comforts like certainty does.
— Amit Kalantri

I buy my clothes large, so I feel comfortable gaining weight.
— Jarod Kintz

Cozy

Sanity is a cozy lie.
— Susan Sontag

It's the best feeling when you wake up and it's warm and cozy, and you don't have to go to work.
— Emmy Rossum

Easygoing

I am generally a very happy and easygoing person. It's always better to meet people with a smile rather than looking cold, especially when you first meet. It changes everything.
— Heidi Klum

Conversion is not the smooth, easygoing process some men seem to think... It is wounding work, this breaking of the hearts, but without wounding there is no saving.
— John Bunyan

Familiar

No one realizes how beautiful it is to travel until he comes home and rests his head on his old, familiar pillow.
— Lin Yutang

And yet, when everything is alien the alien becomes familiar.
— Matt Haig

Email is very informal, a memo.
But I find that not signing off or
not having a salutation bothers me.
— Judith Martin

I'm a pretty informal guy. I ride
a Harley.
— Francis Collins

Informal

Honey, no offense, but sometimes I
think I could shoot you and watch
you kick.
— Raymond Carver

It's funny how intimate it feels to
get a text.
— Sophie Ellis Bextor

Intimate

My perfect guy wears converse, is
totally laid-back, and doesn't worry
about being cool.
— Selena Gomez

Although being laid-back and relax
can also lead to creativity, mostly it
means that nothing much gets done.
— Donald Norman

Laid-back

Ice cream is the perfect buffer,
because you can do things in a
somewhat lighthearted way. People
have an emotional response to ice
cream. Caring, and eating is a powerful combination.
— Jerry Greenfield

It's funny because being comedic
and happy and lighthearted is who
I am as a person, so they're easier
emotions for me to connect with.
— Lindsay Lohan

Lighthearted

Loose

I think if you are going to be with someone for a while, you really need someone you can let loose with and let go of all the stress of the day.
— Matt Lanter

All our words from loose using have lost their edge.
— Ernest Hemingway

Low-key

One important reason to stay calm is that calm parents hear more. Low-key, accepting parents are the ones whose children keep talking.
— Mary Pipher

Some of your worst gangsters are guys who were very low-key.
— Mickey Rourke

Mellow

Mellow nuts have the hardest rind.
— Sir Walter Scott

They call me mellow yellow.
— Donovan

Nonchalant

I love New York. You can pop out of the Underworld in Central Park, hail a taxi, head down Fifth Avenue with a giant hellhound loping behind you, and nobody even looks at you funny.
— Rick Riordan

I have often said that I wish I had invented blue jeans: the most spectacular, the most practical, the most relaxed and nonchalant.
— Yves Saint-Laurent

The light music of whisky falling into
glasses made an agreeable interlude.
— James Joyce

Relaxed

A little nonsense now and then, is
cherished by the wisest men.
— Roald Dahl

Everything should be made as
simple as possible, but not simpler.
— Albert Einstein

Unfussy

My goal is no longer to get more
done, but rather to have less to do.
— Francine Jay

A person who makes a fire of straw
has much smoke but little warmth.
— Vikrant Parsai

Warm

There's no better feeling in the
world than a warm pizza box on
your lap.
— Kevin James

Ceaseless

Adamant

People are adamant learning is
not just looking at a Google page.
But it is.
— Sugata Mitra

I have to get a licence to drive a
motorcycle to protect myself and the
people around me. I am adamant
there should be some sort of licens-
ing required to have children.
— Tim Allen

Day and night

There is only one day left, always
starting over: it is given to us at dawn
and taken away from us at dusk.
— Jean-Paul Sartre

In this age of 24/7 headlines, the term
'newsweekly' seems almost quaint.
— Graydon Carter

Fanatical

One arrives at style only with
atrocious effort, with fanatical
and devoted stubbornness.
— Gustave Flaubert

Good habits are worth being fanatical about.
— John Irving

Intense

I also have intense relationships
with furniture... probably because
we practically had none when I
was growing up.
— Barbra Streisand

I mean, I love winning, but losing is
a much more intense feeling.
— Jennie Finch

It's a non-stop invention, this
game of life, and as soon as you
think you've got it, you lose it.
— Tim Finn

Nonstop

Me, Billy Crystal and John Good-
man hang out non-stop, and all we
do is silly voices. We hang out in a
little closet and do voices together.
— Bobby Moynihan

I've known lots of people that
are talented and nothing happens. It's not about talent, it's
relentless drive.
— Julie Brown

Relentless

History is a relentless master.
It has no present, only the past
rushing into the future. To try
to hold fast is to be swept aside.
— John F. Kennedy

Work is a necessity for man.
Man invented the alarm clock.
— Pablo Picasso

Round the clock

The peculiar combination of joy and
sadness in bell music - both of clock
chimes, and of change-ringing.
— A. N. Wilson

Accessible - Creative

Celebrated

Accomplished

There is joy in work. There is no happiness except in the realization that we have accomplished something.
— Henry Ford

Nothing great in the world has ever been accomplished without passion.
— Georg Wilhelm Friedrich Hegel

Big
(see page 49)

Big results require big ambitions.
— Heraclitus

Speak softly and carry a big stick; you will go far.
— Theodore Roosevelt

Excessive

Excessive sorrow laughs. Excessive joy weeps.
— William Blake

There is nothing more imprudent than excessive prudence.
— Charles Caleb Colton

Famous

I pretended to be somebody I wanted to be until finally I became that person. Or he became me.
— Cary Grant

For famous men have the whole earth as their memorial.
— Pericles

Controversial proposals, once accepted, soon become hallowed.
— Dean Acheson

I'm in a hallowed league of artists.
— Q-Tip

Hallowed

To be ignorant of the lives of the most celebrated men of antiquity is to continue in a state of childhood all our days.
— Plutarch

Go where you're celebrated, not tolerated. I'm celebrated in Detroit.
— Kid Rock

Iconic

I tread in the footsteps of illustrious men... in receiving from the people the sacred trust confided to my illustrious predecessor.
— Martin Van Buren

The martyr cannot be dishonored. Every lash inflicted is a tongue of fame; every prison a more illustrious abode.
— Ralph Waldo Emerson

Illustrious

You can't get un-famous. You can get infamous, but you can't get un-famous.
— Dave Chappelle

It doesn't matter if you're famous or infamous. All that matters is you're a celebrity.
— Willie Geist

Infamous

Legendary

I'd say Juventus has a story as legendary as the Yankees.
— Lapo Elkann

I'ma continue to make records, continue to make hits, continue to be what I am, legendary.
— Young Jeezy

Matchless

Who can work this matchless strength. Where shall he find.
— Ralph Waldo Emerson

Just as the body cannot exist without blood, so the soul needs the matchless and pure strength of faith.
— Mahatma Gandhi

Memorable

Good design is making something intelligible and memorable. Great design is making something memorable and meaningful.
— Dieter Rams

What makes things memorable is that they are meaningful, significant, colorful.
— Joshua Foer

Peerless

The more you like yourself, the less you are like anyone else, which makes you unique.
— Walt Disney

Certain brief sentences are peerless in their ability to give one the feeling that nothing remains to be said.
— Jean Rostand

Charming

Absorbing

While the spoken word can travel faster, you can't take it home in your hand. Only the written word can be absorbed wholly at the convenience of the reader.
— Kingman Brewster, Jr.

It is a cursed evil to any man to become as absorbed in any subject as I am in mine.
— Charles Darwin

Admirable

There is only one admirable form of the imagination: the imagination that is so intense that it creates a new reality, that it makes things happen.
— Sean O'Faolain

I admire Shakespeare enormously. But since I can't be him, I'm glad that his marriage was unhappy and he's dead.
— Bauvard

Adorable

I'm tired of all this nonsense about beauty being skin deep. That's deep enough. What do you want, an adorable pancreas?
— Jean Kerr

When grace is joined with wrinkles, it is adorable. There is an unspeakable dawn in happy old age.
— Victor Hugo

People who throw kisses
are hopelessly lazy.
— Bob Hope

Affectionate

I've always wanted male friends
that I could be real intimate with
and talk about important things
with and be as affectionate with that
person as I would be with a girl.
— Kurt Cobain

Fantastic tyrant of the amorous
heart. How hard thy yoke, how cruel
thy dart. Those escape your anger
who refuse your sway, and those are
punished most, who most obey.
— Matthew Prior

Amorous

At the touch of love everyone
becomes a poet.
— Plato

When a woman gets dressed up to go
out at night, she wants to give 50%
away, and hold the rest back. If you're
an open book, there's no allure.
— Alexander McQueen

Alluring

In 1976, Jimmy Carter - peanut
farmer; carried his own suitcase,
imagine that. By 1980, ordinariness
in high office had lost its allure.
— George Will

Charisma only wins people's attention.
Once you have their attention, you
have to have something to tell them.
— Daniel Quinn

Charismatic

The reason we're successful, darling?
My overall charisma, of course.
— Freddie Mercury

Dashing

The painter who feels obligated to depict his subjects as uniformly beautiful or handsome and without flaws will fall short of making art.
— Joyce Maynard

Love thy neighbor - and if he happens to be tall, debonair and devastating, it will be that much easier.
— Mae West

Delightful

We want to do a lot of stuff; we're not in great shape. We didn't get a good night's sleep. We're a little depressed. Coffee solves all these problems in one delightful little cup.
— Jerry Seinfeld

What a delightful thing is the conversation of specialists! One understands absolutely nothing and it's charming.
— Edgar Degas

Disarming

If we could read the secret history of our enemies we should find in each man's life sorrow and suffering enough to disarm all hostility.
— Henry Wadsworth Longfellow

I think romance is anything honest. As long as it's honest, it's so disarming.
— Kristen Stewart

Life every man holds dear; but
the dear man holds honor far
more precious dear than life.
— William Shakespeare

Most cynics are really crushed
romantics: they've been hurt, they're
sensitive, and their cynicism is a
shell that's protecting this tiny, dear
part in them that's still alive.
— Jeff Bridges

Dear

In the old days, a con man
would be good looking, suave,
well dressed, well spoken and
presented themselves real well.
Those days are gone.
— Frank Abagnale

I felt only as a man can feel who
is roaming over the prairies of the
far West, well armed, and mounted
on a fleet and gallant steed.
— Buffalo Bill

Debonair

Eloquence, at its highest pitch, leaves
little room for reason or reflection,
but addresses itself entirely captivating the willing hearers, and subduing
their understanding.
— David Hume

There was something terribly
enthralling in the exercise of influence. No other activity was like it.
— Oscar Wilde

Enthralling

Fascinating

Being good in business is the most fascinating kind of art. Making money is art and working is art and good business is the best art.
— Andy Warhol

What's so fascinating and frustrating and great about life is that you're constantly starting over, all the time, and I love that.
— Billy Crystal

Funny
(see page 227)

A joke is a very serious thing.
— Winston Churchill

A sense of humor is a major defense against minor troubles.
— Mignon McLaughlin

Lovable

I like to think that my arrogance, impetuosity, impatience, selfishness and greed are the qualities that make me the lovable chap I am.
— Richard Hammond

Authors like cats because they are such quiet, lovable, wise creatures, and cats like authors for the same reasons.
— Robertson Davies

Lovely

I think that I shall never see a poem lovely as a tree.
— Joyce Kilmer

Um... Bulgaria is an interesting country. The people are lovely.
— Rachel Nichols

Listening is a magnetic and strange
thing, a creative force. The friends
who listen to us are the ones we
move toward.
— Karl A. Menninger

A magnetic personality doesn't
necessarily indicate a good heart.
— Laura Linney

Magnetic

Politeness [is] a sign of dignity,
not subservience.
— Theodore Roosevelt

When you have to kill a man,
it costs nothing to be polite.
— Winston Churchill

Polite

I remember a hundred lovely lakes,
and the fragrant breath of pine and
fir and cedar and poplar trees. The
trail has strung upon it, as upon a
thread of silk, opalescent dawns and
saffron sunsets.
— Hamlin Garland

I don't like silk underwear.
They don't do the job, you know?
— Matt LeBlanc

Silky

I come from Detroit where it's rough
and I'm not a smooth talker.
— Eminem

I try to dress smooth, I try to keep
my face shaved, I try to keep my
head cut. I try to do all the things to
keep it smooth going!
— J. B. Smoove

Smooth

Revenge is sweet and not fattening.
— Alfred Hitchcock

Sweet

Heard melodies are sweet, but those
unheard are sweeter.
— John Keats

Clear

Brief

Life is often compared to a marathon, but I think it is more like being a sprinter; long stretches of hard work punctuated by brief moments in which we are given the opportunity to perform at our best.
— Michael Johnson

To be brief is almost a condition of being inspired.
— George Santayana

Concise

In labouring to be concise, I become obscure.
— Horace

Vigorous writing is concise. A sentence should contain no unnecessary words, a paragraph no unnecessary sentences, for the same reason that a drawing should have no unnecessary lines.
— William Strunk, Jr.

Concrete

No problem can be solved until it is reduced to some simple form. The changing of a vague difficulty into a specific, concrete form is a very essential element in thinking.
— J. P. Morgan

The city is not a concrete jungle, it is a human zoo.
— Desmond Morris

Crisp

Lettuce is like conversation; it must be fresh and crisp, so sparkling that you scarcely notice the bitter in it.
— Charles Dudley Warner

Less really is more. I think you've got to keep it short, crisp and clean.
— Brad Thor

When people are crystal clear about
the most important priorities not
only are they many times more productive, they discover they have the
time they need to have a whole life.
— Stephen Covey

What Youth deemed crystal,
Age finds out was dew.
— Robert Browning

Crystal

Sometimes I wonder if we shall ever
grow up in our politics and say definite things which mean something, or
whether we shall always go on using
generalities which mean very little.
— Eleanor Roosevelt

All the evolution we know of pro-
ceeds from the vague to the definite.
— Charles Sanders Peirce

Definite

Hundreds of butterflies flitted in
and out of sight like short-lived
punctuation marks in a stream of
consciousness without beginning
or end.
— Haruki Murakami

Science is descriptive, not prescrip-
tive; it can tell us about causes but
it cannot tell us about purposes.
— Jonathan Sacks

Descriptive

Accessible - Creative

Direct

Great ambition is the passion of a great character. Those endowed with it may perform very good or very bad acts. All depends on the principles which direct them.
— Napoleon Bonaparte

We cannot direct the wind, but we can adjust the sails.
— Dolly Parton

Distinct

Remember my mantra: distinct... or extinct.
— Tom Peters

There are two distinct classes of what are called thoughts: those that we produce in ourselves by reflection and the act of thinking and those that bolt into the mind of their own accord.
— Thomas Paine

Factual

A documentary photograph is not a factual photograph.
— Dorothea Lange

I don't believe that narrative works when it's trying to teach a lesson or speak a factual truth.
— Shane Carruth

I'm a forthright person and I am
ambitious and I do hope that I get
to do more, interesting work but
not at the expense of me not being
who I am.
— Jessica Clark

The tragedy of bold, forthright,
industrious people is that they act so
continuously without much thinking,
that it becomes dry and empty.
— Brenda Ueland

Forthright

It is important to our friends to
believe that we are unreservedly
frank with them, and important
to friendship that we are not.
— Mignon McLaughlin

Frank and explicit - that is the right
line to take when you wish to conceal your own mind and confuse the
minds of others.
— Benjamin Disraeli

Frank

Accessible - Creative

Tricks and treachery are the practice of fools, that don't have brains
enough to be honest.
— Benjamin Franklin

A person should not be too honest.
Straight trees are cut first and hon-
est people are screwed first.
— Chanakya

Honest
(see page 267)

Lucid

I'm not particularly lucid after a concert. I'm not very lucid before, either.
— Leonard Slatkin

I would describe myself as quite sane and lucid, which is why I'm still alive.
— John McAfee

Matter-of-fact

Sincerity is moral truth.
— George Henry Lewes

My psychiatrist told me I was crazy and I said I want a second opinion. He said okay, you're ugly too.
— Rodney Dangerfield

Narrative

Sometimes, a novel is like a train: the first chapter is a comfortable seat in an attractive carriage, and the narrative speeds up. But there are other sorts of trains, and other sorts of novels.
— Jane Smiley

Narrative identity takes part in the story's movement, in the dialectic between order and disorder.
— Paul Ricoeur

Obvious

It has become appallingly obvious that our technology has exceeded our humanity.
— Albert Einstein

A day without sunshine is like, you know, night.
— Steve Martin

Antarctica is otherworldly, like nothing I've ever seen before. Stark, cold, beautiful desolation.
— Mark Hoppus

Airline travel is hours of boredom interrupted by moments of stark terror.
— Al Boliska

Stark

Juggling is very, very straightforward; very, very black and white; you're manipulating objects, not people. And that's always appealed to me.
— Penn Jillette

Nothing more completely baffles one who is full of trick and duplicity, than straightforward and simple integrity in another.
— Charles Caleb Colton

Straightforward

Brevity is the soul of wit.
— William Shakespeare

Like all sweet dreams, it will be brief, but brevity makes sweetness, doesn't it?
— Stephen King

Succinct

If malice or envy were tangible and had a shape, it would be the shape of a boomerang.
— Charley Reese

I don't think I'm tangible to myself.
— Bob Dylan

Tangible

Terse

Don't confuse being stimulating
with being blunt.
— Barbara Walters

At first I probably seem very abrupt,
but I like efficiency. There's work
and there's play, and I always think:
'Let's get the work over with so we
can thoroughly enjoy the play.'
— Kathy Reichs

Tidy

Be careless in your dress if you will,
but keep a tidy soul.
— Mark Twain

You don't have to live on a farm to
have chickens; in some places, you
just need a little bit of green space
and a tidy chicken coop.
— Amy Robach

Transparent

There's no sense talking about priorities. Priorities reveal themselves.
We're all transparent against the
face of the clock.
— Eric Zorn

When you grow up in a family of
languages, you develop a kind of
casual fluency, so that languages,
though differently colored, all seem
transparent to experience.
— David Antin

Accessible - Creative

Compassionate

Accepting

It is the mark of an educated mind to be able to entertain a thought without accepting it.
— Aristotle

There's a need for accepting responsibility - for a person's life and making choices that are not just ones for immediate short-term comfort.
— Buzz Aldrin

Caring

From caring comes courage.
— Lao Tzu

What's powerful about a love scene is not seeing the act. It's seeing the passion, the need, the desire, the caring, the fear.
— Patrick Swayze

Fatherly

When a father gives to his son, both laugh; when a son gives to his father, both cry.
— William Shakespeare

My father was my teacher. But most importantly he was a great dad.
— Beau Bridges

Grateful

I am grateful to be a woman. I must have done something great in another life.
— Maya Angelou

Life is hard. Then you die. Then they throw dirt in your face. Then the worms eat you. Be grateful it happens in that order.
— David Gerrold

To be meek, patient, tactful, modest, honorable, brave, is not to be
either manly or womanly; it is to
be humane.
— Jane Harrison

We're so much more likely to
feel sympathy for an animal than
another person; thus, the best fiction uses animals to define
truly humane behavior.
— Chuck Palahniuk

Humane

Not only do I think being nice and
kind is easy, but being kind, in my
opinion, is important.
— Dwayne Johnson

History will be kind to me for
I intend to write it.
— Winston Churchill

Kind

It is straightforward for me to
be ethical, responsible, and
kind-hearted because I have the
resources to support that.
— Edward Tufte

Carry out a random act of kindness,
with no expectation of reward, safe
in the knowledge that one day someone might do the same for you.
— Princess Diana

Kindhearted

Loving

Being deeply loved by someone
gives you strength, while loving
someone deeply gives you courage.
— Lao Tzu

I am happier when I love than when
I am loved. I adore my husband, my
son, my grandchildren, my mother,
my dog, and frankly, I don't know if
they even like me. But who cares?
— Isabel Allende

Motherly

Biology is the least of what makes
someone a mother.
— Oprah Winfrey

My mother gave lots of good advice
and had a lot to say. As you get
older, you realize everything she
said was true.
— Lenny Kravitz

Tolerant

The public is wonderfully tolerant.
It forgives everything except genius.
— Oscar Wilde

Nothing makes you more tolerant
of a neighbor's noisy party than
being there.
— Franklin P. Jones

Thankful

I did not break up the Beatles. If
you're going to blame me for breaking the Beatles up, you should be
thankful that I made them into myth
rather than a crumbling group.
— Yoko Ono

I am thankful for laughter, except
when milk comes out of my nose.
— Woody Allen

It takes a tough man to make
a tender chicken.
— Frank Perdue

In a separation it is the one who is
not really in love who says the more
tender things.
— Marcel Proust

Tender

I really just want to be warm yellow
light that pours over everyone I love.
— Conor Oberst

A house that does not have one
warm, comfy chair in it is soulless.
— Mary Sarton

Warm

Confident

Aggressive

All dogs can become aggressive, but the difference between an aggressive Chihuahua and an aggressive pit bull is that the pit bull can do more damage.
— Cesar Millan

Aggressive, tough and defiant may describe me, but that leaves the impression I'm mean and I'm not.
— Joan Jett

Ambitious

The very substance of the ambitious is merely the shadow of a dream.
— William Shakespeare

I'm tough, ambitious, and I know exactly what I want.
— Madonna

Bold

Freedom lies in being bold.
— Robert Frost

Originality implies being bold enough to go beyond accepted norms.
— Anthony Storr

Brave

The real man smiles in trouble, gathers strength from distress, and grows brave by reflection.
— Thomas Paine

I learned that courage was not the absence of fear, but the triumph over it.
— Nelson Mandela

I am certain of nothing but the
holiness of the heart's affections,
and the truth of imagination.
— John Keats

To believe with certainty we must
begin with doubting.
— Stanislaus I

Certain

Well-timed silence is the most
commanding expression.
— Mark Helprin

He was very commanding, and you
had to know what you were doing to
work for Mr. Rogers.
— Glenn Ford

Commanding

He who is not courageous enough to
take risks will accomplish nothing
in life.
— Muhammad Ali

A timid person is frightened before
a danger, a coward during the time,
and a courageous person afterward.
— Jean Paul

Courageous
(see page 123)

Making good decisions is a crucial
skill at every level.
— Peter Drucker

One man can be a crucial ingredi-
ent on a team, but one man cannot
make a team.
— Kareem Abdul-Jabbar

Crucial

Accessible - Creative

Decisive

Pursue one great decisive aim with force and determination.
— Carl von Clausewitz

When I take action, I'm not going to fire a $2 million missile at a $10 empty tent and hit a camel in the butt. It's going to be decisive.
— George W. Bush

Deliberate

I am deliberate and afraid of nothing.
— Audre Lorde

The people themselves, and not their servants, can safely reverse their own deliberate decisions.
— Abraham Lincoln

Emphatic

I answer in the affirmative with an emphatic 'No.'
— Boyle Roche

The most emphatic place in a clause or sentence is the end.
— F. L. Lucas

Fearless

I think fearless is having fears but jumping anyway.
— Taylor Swift

Fate loves the fearless.
— James Russell Lowell

We're a bit flashy, but the music's
not one big noise.
— Freddie Mercury

The motto is always 'flashy but
classy.' You've got to be original and
stand out from the crowd and take
some chances. But you've always got
to keep it classy.
— Mayer Hawthorne

Flashy

Only those who will risk going
too far can possibly find out how
far one can go.
— T. S. Eliot

Courage is being scared to death...
and saddling up anyway.
— John Wayne

Gutsy

If you ask me what I came into this
life to do, I will tell you: I came to
live out loud.
— Emile Zola

Everything becomes a little different as soon as it is spoken out loud.
— Hermann Hesse

Loud

Comedy is actually very macho driven.
— Scott Thompson

All girls like guys who are tough.
— Marisa Miller

Macho

Positive
(see page 389)

Once you replace negative thoughts with positive ones, you'll start having positive results.
— Willie Nelson

Positive anything is better than negative nothing.
— Elbert Hubbard

Proud

We will always remember. We will always be proud. We will always be prepared, so we will always be free.
— Ronald Reagan

I'm a black American, I am proud of my race. I am proud of who I am. I have a lot of pride and dignity.
— Michael Jackson

Resolute

The truest wisdom is a resolute determination.
— Napoleon Bonaparte

Generally speaking, the way of the warrior is resolute acceptance of death.
— Miyamoto Musashi

Reverent

An unimaginative person can neither be reverent or kind.
— John Ruskin

To keep the heart unwrinkled, to be hopeful, kindly, cheerful, reverent that is to triumph over old age.
— Amos Bronson Alcott

Solitary trees, if they grow at all, grow strong.
— Winston Churchill

Solitary

Sometimes the solitary voice can be the best one.
— Frank Miller

Once I'm committed, I'm unafraid of the outcome.
— Helmut Lang

Unafraid

The flower has opened, has been in the sun and is unafraid. I'm taking more chances; I'm bold and proud.
— Paula Cole

Cooperative

Collaborative

Unity is strength... when there is teamwork and collaboration, wonderful things can be achieved.
— Mattie Stepanek

Art is a collaboration between God and the artist, and the less the artist does the better.
— Andre Gide

Collective

Unions are about the collective leverage, the power of numbers versus the power of capital.
— Kevin O'Leary

Reality is nothing but a collective hunch.
— Lily Tomlin

Communal

Communal well-being is central to human life.
— Cat Stevens

I hardly ever go into the studio with a work complete in my head. It emerges from communal activity.
— Brian Eno

Constructive

You must not under any pretense allow your mind to dwell on any thought that is not positive, constructive, optimistic, kind.
— Emmet Fox

Human nature is potentially aggressive and destructive and potentially orderly and constructive.
— Margaret Mead

I have cherished the ideal of a democratic and free society in which all
persons live together in harmony
and with equal opportunities.
— Nelson Mandela

The health of a democratic society
may be measured by the quality
of functions performed by private
citizens.
— Alexis de Tocqueville

Democratic

Successful diplomacy is an align-
ment of objectives and means.
— Dennis Ross

I would like to be George Clooney
diplomatic. I just don't have the
wherewithal yet or the inner
serenity.
— Shia LaBeouf

Diplomatic

A formally harmonious product
needs no decoration; it should be
elevated through pure form.
— Ferdinand Porsche

Imagine what a harmonious world
it could be if every single person,
both young and old shared a little
of what he is good at doing.
— Quincy Jones

Harmonious

If the human race wishes to have a
prolonged and indefinite period of
material prosperity, they have only
got to behave in a peaceful and helpful way toward one another.
— Winston Churchill

I am the most helpful and open up
doors for everyone and I like to share.
— Arnold Schwarzenegger

Helpful

Synergetic

I truly believe in positive synergy,
that your positive mindset gives you
a more hopeful outlook, and belief
that you can do something great
means you will do something great.
— Russell Wilson

I still believe in synergy, but I call it
natural law.
— Barry Diller

United

To be one, to be united is a great thing.
— Bono

The United States needed a civil war
to unite properly.
— Umberto Eco

Courageous

Adventurous

I feel very adventurous. There are
so many doors to be opened, and
I'm not afraid to look behind them.
— Elizabeth Taylor

I'm more of an adventurous type
than a relationship type.
— Bob Dylan

Brave

Electric communication will
never be a substitute for the face
of someone who with their soul
encourages another person to be
brave and true.
— Charles Dickens

A hero is no braver than an
ordinary man, but he is brave five
minutes longer.
— Ralph Waldo Emerson

Chivalrous

The motto of chivalry is also the
motto of wisdom; to serve all, but
love only one.
— Honore de Balzac

Some say that the age of chivalry is
past, that the spirit of romance is
dead. The age of chivalry is never
past, so long as there is a wrong left
unredressed on earth.
— Charles Kingsley

Daring

All serious daring starts from within.
— Eudora Welty

Daring ideas are like chessmen
moved forward; they may be beaten,
but they may start a winning game.
— Johann Wolfgang von Goethe

I am not fearless. I get scared plenty.
But I have also learned how to chan-
nel that emotion to sharpen me.
— Bear Grylls

I'm fearless, I don't complain. Even
when horrible things happen to me,
I go on.
— Sofia Vergara

Fearless

Real relationship is gritty and earthy,
the stuff that life is made of.
— Amy Grant

New Yorkers are real gritty and tough.
— Ray Kelly

Gritty

Anybody with a little guts and the
desire to apply himself can make it,
he can make anything he wants to
make of himself.
— Willie Shoemaker

Talent is helpful in writing, but guts
are absolutely necessary.
— Jessamyn West

Gusty

I think that we all do heroic things,
but hero is not a noun, it's a verb.
— Robert Downey, Jr.

When we quit thinking primarily
about ourselves and our own self-pres-
ervation, we undergo a truly heroic
transformation of consciousness.
— Joseph Campbell

Heroic
(see page 259)

Intrepid

It is very perplexing how an intrepid frontier people, who fought a wilderness, floods, tornadoes, and the Rockies, cower before criticism, which is regarded as a malignant tumor in the imagination.
— Edward Dahlberg

Intrepid, unprincipled, reckless, predatory, with boundless ambition, civilized in externals but a savage at heart, America is, or may yet be, the Paul Jones of nations.
— Herman Melville

Red-blooded

Baseball is a red-blooded sport for red-blooded men. It's no pink tea, and mollycoddles had better stay out. It's a struggle for supremacy, a survival of the fittest.
— Ty Cobb

Sure, I did a lot of things in excess. But if you look at the core, the foundation of what I pursued, what red-blooded young American male in my position wouldn't?
— Charlie Sheen

Strong
(see page 449)

A woman is like a tea bag - you can't tell how strong she is until you put her in hot water.
— Eleanor Roosevelt

The world breaks everyone, and afterward, some are strong at the broken places.
— Ernest Hemingway

To be one's self, and unafraid
whether right or wrong, is more
admirable than the easy cowardice
of surrender to conformity.
— Irving Wallace

Once I'm committed, I'm unafraid of
the outcome.
— Helmut Lang

Unafraid

Courageous and Creative

Creative

Artistic

The purpose of art is washing the dust of daily life off our souls.
— Pablo Picasso

The aim of art is to represent not the outward appearance of things, but their inward significance.
— Aristotle

Colorful

What makes things memorable is that they are meaningful, significant, colorful.
— Joshua Foer

If you're quiet, you're not living. You've got to be noisy and colorful and lively.
— Mel Brooks

Crafty

The crafty rabbit has three different entrances to its lair.
— Chinese Proverb

Behind closed doors, I'm a crafty person.
— Raven-Symoné

Curious

When you're curious, you find lots of interesting things to do.
— Walt Disney

I have no special talent. I am only passionately curious.
— Albert Einstein

The future has already arrived. It's
just not evenly distributed yet.
— William Gibson

Like a ribbon of weed I am flung far
every time the door opens.
— Virginia Woolf

Far-flung

A clever, imaginative, humorous
request can open closed doors and
closed minds.
— Percy Ross

The most imaginative people are the
most credulous, for them everything
is possible.
— Alexander Chase

Imaginative

It will be found, in fact, that the
ingenious are always fanciful, and
the truly imaginative never otherwise than analytic.
— Edgar Allan Poe

He is the best physician who is the
most ingenious inspirer of hope.
— Samuel Taylor Coleridge

Ingenious

If you're not failing every now and
again, it's a sign you're not doing
anything very innovative.
— Woody Allen

Predicting innovation is something
of a self-canceling exercise: the
most probable innovations are probably the least innovative.
— P. J. O'Rourke

Innovative
(see page 299)

Instinctive

We are much more willing to admit that certain things are completely instinctive and others are really intellectual.
— Rem Koolhaas

You've got to go with what feels instinctive and true to your heart, and filter out all of the other stuff.
— Alison Goldfrapp

Inventive

Invention, it must be humbly admitted, does not consist in creating out of void, but out of chaos.
— Mary Wollstonecraft Shelley

I never did anything by accident, nor did any of my inventions come by accident; they came by work.
— Thomas A. Edison

Inquisitive

Cats are inquisitive, but hate to admit it.
— Mason Cooley

There's nothing that can help you understand your beliefs more than trying to explain them to an inquisitive child.
— Frank A. Clark

Make-shift

Nothing can ever happen twice. In consequence, the sorry fact is that we arrive here improvised and leave without the chance to practice.
— Wislawa Szymborska

You can really taste the difference between a shop-bought and a good homemade mayo.
— Yotam Ottolenghi

Every great architect is - necessarily
- a great poet. He must be a great
original interpreter of his time, his
day, his age.
— Frank Lloyd Wright

Be yourself. The world worships
the original.
— Ingrid Bergman

Original

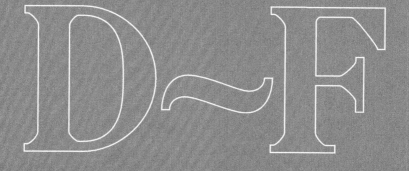

Detailed

Accurate

The power of accurate observation is commonly called cynicism by those who have not got it.
— George Bernard Shaw

There is no substitute for accurate knowledge. Know yourself, know your business, know your men.
— Lee Iacocca

Careful

You've got to be very careful if you don't know where you are going, because you might not get there.
— Yogi Berra

If you are careful with people, they will offer you part of themselves. That is the big secret.
— Eve Arnold

Cautious

I prefer to be alive, so I'm cautious about taking risks.
— Werner Herzog

We are optimistic, but we are optimistic in a cautious fashion.
— Tom Lantos

Comprehensive

Let your discourse with men of business be short and comprehensive.
— George Washington

In the design process, there's a need to be culturally comprehensive.
— Dries van Noten

When you have collected all the
facts and fears and made your
decision, turn off all your fears
and go ahead!
— George S. Patton

A little and a little, collected
together, becomes a great deal;
the heap in the barn consists of
single grains, and drop and drop
make the inundation.
— Saadi

Collected

A language is an exact reflection
of the character and growth of
its speakers.
— Cesar Chavez

Reading maketh a full man; con-
ference a ready man; and writing
an exact man.
— Francis Bacon

Exact

Without claiming to be exhaustive, I
maintain that every philosophy repro-
duces within itself, in one way or
another, the conflict in which it finds
itself compromised and caught up in
the outside world.
— Louis Althusser

...when the exhaustive exegesis of
God's Word doesn't create people
transformed into the image of Jesus,
we have missed the forest for the trees.
— Jen Hatmaker

Exhaustive

Incisive

I don't dawdle. I'm a surgeon. I make an incision, do what needs to be done and sew up the wound. There is a beginning, a middle and an end.
— Dr. Richard Selzer

I would much prefer to suffer from the clean incision of an honest lancet than from a sweetened poison.
— Mark Twain

Methodical

Education is the methodical creation of the habit of thinking.
— Ernest Dimnet

Pilots are very methodical and meticulous, and artists tend not to be.
— Chris Carter

Optimal

Every situation is an opportunity to be your best.
— Rosalene Glickman

Well I believe in the desirability of an optimal society.
— Tom Stoppard

Precise

Be precise. A lack of precision is dangerous when the margin of error is small.
— Donald Rumsfeld

When a company owns one precise thought in the consumer's mind, it sets the context for everything and there should be no distinction between brand, product, service and experience.
— Maurice Saatchi

Science is the systematic classification of experience.
— George Henry Lewes

Let us mobilize all our resources in a systematic and organized way and tackle the grave issues that confront us with grim determination and discipline worthy of a great nation.
— Muhammad Ali Jinnah

Systematic

There is no short cut to achievement. Life requires thorough preparation - veneer isn't worth anything.
— George Washington Carver

The only fence against the world is a thorough knowledge of it.
— John Locke

Thorough

It does not take a majority to prevail... but rather an irate, tireless minority, keen on setting brushfires of freedom in the minds of men.
— Samuel Adams

Teachers are out there with a very difficult job, which they pursue with tireless dedication.
— Chi McBride

Tireless

Never neglect details. When everyone's mind is dulled or distracted the leader must be doubly vigilant.
— Colin Powell

Be vigilant, for nothing one achieves lasts forever.
— Tahar Ben Jelloun

Vigilant

Wakeful

One must exercise proper delibera-
tion, plan carefully before making a
move, and be alert in guarding against
relapse following a renaissance.
— Horace

Hope is the dream of a waking man.
— Pliny the Elder

Dynamic

Adaptable

I don't think of myself as unbreakable. Perhaps I'm just rather flexible and adaptable.
— Aung San Suu Kyi

You can't build an adaptable organization without adaptable people - and individuals change only when they have to, or when they want to.
— Gary Hamel

Alive

Today you are you! That is truer than true! There is no one alive who is you-er than you!
— Dr. Seuss

You are either alive and proud or you are dead, and when you are dead, you can't care anyway.
— Steven Biko

Animated

Today a new sun rises for me; everything lives, everything is animated, everything seems to speak to me of my passion, everything invites me to cherish it.
— Ninon de L'Enclos

I'd love to be animated. I've always wanted to jump off of a bridge and not be hurt, like Bugs Bunny.
— Carrot Top

Avid

I'm an avid supporter of living life to its fullest and not always waiting for tomorrow.
— Teri Polo

Love is an eloquent speaker and I the avid listener.
— Dodinsky

A consistent soul believes in destiny,
a capricious one in chance.
— Benjamin Disraeli

Lightning is such a capricious
instrument.
— William Tweed

Capricious

Innovation is all about people. Innovation thrives when the population
is diverse, accepting and willing
to cooperate.
— Vivek Wadhwa

I like to think that as long as you
continue choosing diverse roles, you
can avoid becoming predictable.
— Christian Bale

Diverse

To him whose elastic and vigorous
thought keeps pace with the sun,
the day is a perpetual morning.
— Henry David Thoreau

The elastic heart of youth cannot
be compressed into one constrained
shape long at a time.
— Mark Twain

Elastic

Had I become a priest, the sermons
would've been electric!
— Johnny Vegas

Enthusiasm is the electricity of life.
How do you get it? You act enthusi-
astic until you make it a habit.
— Gordon Parks

Electric

Detailed - Funny

Energetic

In this very real world, good
doesn't drive out evil. Evil doesn't
drive out good. But the energetic
displaces the passive.
— Bill Bernbach

I'm much more energetic now;
you might say live performance
is my mission.
— John Fogerty

Energizing

Optimism with some experience
behind it is much more energizing
than plain old experience with a
certain degree of cynicism.
— Twyla Tharp

Super-ambitious goals tend to be
unifying and energizing to people;
but only if they believe there's a
chance of success.
— Peter Diamandis

Flexible

Stay committed to your decisions,
but stay flexible in your approach.
— Tony Robbins

Nothing is softer or more flexible
than water, yet nothing can resist it.
— Lao Tzu

Fluent

I never had dreamed of such a motion,
fluent and graceful, and ambient, soft
as the breeze flitting over the flowers,
but swift as the summer lightning.
— Richard Blackmore

Talking is one of the fine arts - the
noblest, the most important, the most
difficult - and its fluent harmonies
may be spoiled by the intrusion of a
single harsh note.
— Oliver Wendell Holmes

I see music as fluid architecture.
— Joni Mitchell

The goal in life is to be solid, whereas the way that life works is totally fluid, so you can never actually achieve that goal.
— Damien Hirst

Fluid

I'm single, footloose and fancy free, I have no responsibilities, no anchors. Work, friendship and self-improvement, that's me.
— Joel Edgerton

Hey, hey! What's this I see?
I thought this was a party.
LET'S DANCE!
— Ren, from Footloose

Footloose

Our days are a kaleidoscope. Every instant a change takes place. New harmonies, new contrasts, new combinations of every sort.
— Henry Ward Beecher

At the height of laughter, the universe is flung into a kaleidoscope of new possibilities.
— Jean Houston

Kaleidoscopic

I'm so vigorous, and I so take it for granted, because I've always been a real physical person.
— Sally Field

Curiosity is one of the most permanent and certain characteristics of a vigorous intellect.
— Samuel Johnson

Vigorous

Vital

Change is vital, improvement
the logical form of change.
— James Cash Penney

Rap music is the only vital form of
music introduced since punk rock.
— Kurt Cobain

Vivacious

If you're quiet, you're not living.
You've got to be noisy and colorful
and lively.
— Mel Brooks

I'm virile, vigorous, and potent!
— G. Gordon Liddy

Elegant

Aristocratic

An aristocratic culture does not advertise its emotions.
— Johan Huizinga

My tastes are aristocratic, my actions democratic.
— Victor Hugo

Beautiful
(see page 43)

For beautiful eyes, look for the good in others; for beautiful lips, speak only words of kindness; and for poise, walk with the knowledge that you are never alone.
— Audrey Hepburn

The best and most beautiful things in the world cannot be seen or even touched - they must be felt with the heart.
— Helen Keller

Classic

A classic is a book that doesn't have to be written again.
— W. E. B. Du Bois

Proportions are what makes the old Greek temples classic in their beauty.
— Arne Jacobsen

Cultivated

A great architect is not made by way of a brain nearly so much as he is made by way of a cultivated, enriched heart.
— Frank Lloyd Wright

The Japanese say, If the flower is to be beautiful, it must be cultivated.
— Lester Cole

The cultured man is an artist, an artist in humanity.
— Ashley Montagu

A man should be just cultured enough to be able to look with suspicion upon culture at first, not second hand.
— Samuel Butler

Cultured

All labor that uplifts humanity has dignity and importance and should be undertaken with painstaking excellence.
— Martin Luther King, Jr.

The ideal man bears the accidents of life with dignity and grace, making the best of circumstances.
— Aristotle

Dignified

If a man constantly aspires is he not elevated?
— Henry David Thoreau

Culture is the arts elevated to a set of beliefs.
— Thomas Wolfe

Elevated
(see page 163)

We require from buildings two kinds of goodness: first, the doing their practical duty well: then that they be graceful and pleasing in doing it.
— John Ruskin

A graceful taunt is worth a thousand insults.
— Louis Nizer

Graceful

Opulent

The Polo Lounge is like a fine old mink coat: opulent, dignified and warm.
— Bryan Miller

The voice soared majestically, hugely, in the role, flooding the house with opulent, gleaming tones.
— Thor Eckert, Jr.

Polished

A gem cannot be polished without friction, nor a man perfected without trials.
— Lucius Annaeus Seneca

Innocence is like polished armor; it adorns and defends.
— Robert South

Refined

The eye is the most refined of our senses, the one which communicates most directly with our mind, our consciousness.
— Robert Delaunay

The Japanese have a wonderful sense of design and a refinement in their art. They try to produce beautiful paintings with the minimum number of strokes.
— David Rockefeller

Tasteful

Always use tasteful words - you may have to eat them.
— Brennan McGrath

I've always liked Playboy; I think it's very tasteful.
— Trishelle Cannatella

Elevated

Aristocratic

An aristocratic culture does not advertise its emotions.
— Johan Huizinga

The surface of American society is covered with a layer of democratic paint, but from time to time one can see the old aristocratic colours breaking through.
— Alexis de Tocqueville

Chic

My legacy would be that you don't have to give up anything. You can be chic but have a sense of humor, you can be sexy but comfortable, you can be timeless but fresh.
— Michael Kors

I think all girls in the world wish they were a Parisian girl - that sort of effortless chic confidence and comfort in their own skin.
— Natalie Portman

Choice

A man cannot be too careful in the choice of his enemies.
— Oscar Wilde

Two roads diverged in a wood, and I - I took the one less traveled by, And that has made all the difference.
— Robert Frost

Classic

A classic is a book that doesn't have to be written again.
— W. E. B. Du Bois

I'm not trying to be new school and I'm not old school - I'm classic.
— LL Cool J

A girl should be two things: classy
and fabulous.
— Coco Chanel

Classy

A girl knows her limits but a wise
girl knows she has none.
— Marilyn Monroe

I am not an Athenian or a Greek,
but a citizen of the world.
— Socrates

Cosmopolitan

It's a kind of madness in cosmopolitan cities now.
— Sean Connery

It seems unpleasantly refined to put
things off till someone knows.
— William Empson

Couth

Certainly I was relatively a refined
person. No way a tramp.
— Beatrice Wood

The cultured man is an artist, an
artist in humanity.
— Ashley Montagu

Cultured

Culture is the habit of being pleased
with the best and knowing why.
— Henry Van Dyke

I think people think of me as this
elegant person because they always
see me dressed up.
— Vanna White

Dapper

Associate yourself with people of
good quality, for it is better to be
alone than in bad company.
— Booker T. Washington

Deluxe

Creating deluxe cuisine is like playing a sport. Always competitive. Always challenging. And if you slow down a bit, you can no longer return to the top level.
— Joel Robuchon

Maybe my penchant for hippie-deluxe eccentricity came from an escapist dream of a different world. It was tough being a working mom in the 1970s.
— Suzy Menkes

Desirable

All desirable things... are desirable either for the pleasure inherent in themselves, or as a means to the promotion of pleasure and the prevention of pain.
— John Stuart Mill

Design is a constant challenge to balance comfort with luxe, the practical with the desirable.
— Donna Karan

Dignified

All labor that uplifts humanity has dignity and importance and should be undertaken with painstaking excellence.
— Martin Luther King, Jr.

I thought a dignified thing to do would be to live in the country by the time I'm 50 and write books.
— Julian Clary

A discerning eye needs only a hint, and understatement leaves the imagination free to build its own elaborations.
— Russell Page

Discerning

Much madness is divinest sense /
To a discerning eye / Much sense /
The starkest madness.
— Emily Dickinson

Even the wisest woman you talk to is ignorant of something you may know, but an elegant woman never forgets her elegance.
— Oliver Wendell Holmes

Elegant
(see page 155)

A truly elegant taste is generally accompanied with excellency of heart.
— Henry Fielding

Pleasure and action make the hours seem short.
— William Shakespeare

Epicurean

Anyone who's a chef, who loves food, ultimately knows that all that matters is: 'Is it good? Does it give pleasure?'
— Anthony Bourdain

Beauty is the sole ambition, the exclusive goal of taste.
— Charles Baudelaire

Exclusive

The mind gets distracted in all sorts of ways. The heart is its own exclusive concern and diversion.
— Malcolm de Chazal

Detailed - Funny

Exotic

Everyone is so weird in L.A. that if you're somewhat normal, it's exotic.
— David Spade

Most of us, when we go out with a camera in our own country, try to find exotic subject matter to photograph.
— Martin Parr

Extravagant

The great thing about costume jewelry is that there's something for everyone - there are very humorous pieces and very extravagant and outrageous pieces.
— Judith Miller

A miser grows rich by seeming poor; an extravagant man grows poor by seeming rich.
— William Shenstone

Exquisite

Words have no power to impress the mind without the exquisite horror of their reality.
— Edgar Allan Poe

An artist is an artist only because of his exquisite sense of beauty, a sense which shows him intoxicating pleasures, but which at the same time implies and contains an equally exquisite sense of all deformities and all disproportion.
— Charles Baudelaire

I don't like formal gardens. I like
wild nature. It's just the wilderness
instinct in me, I guess.
— Walt Disney

Every company has two organiza-
tional structures: The formal one is
written on the charts; the other is
the everyday relationship of the men
and women in the organization.
— Harold S. Geneen

Formal

It would be very glamorous to be
reincarnated as a great big ring on
Liz Taylor's finger.
— Andy Warhol

For people on the outside, the idea
of going to the White House for a
meeting must seem like the most
important, serious, even glamorous
kind of thing to do.
— Hillary Clinton

Glamorous

Woodstock was both a peaceful
protest and a global celebration.
— Richie Havens

Most religious stories and mytholo-
gies have some sort of similar root,
some sort of global archetypes.
— Maynard James Keenan

Global

Glorious

The most glorious moments in your life are not the so-called days of success, but rather those days when out of dejection and despair you feel rise in you a challenge to life, and the promise of future accomplishments.
— Gustave Flaubert

Let freedom reign. The sun never set on so glorious a human achievement.
— Nelson Mandela

Grand

I have sometimes been wildly, despairingly, acutely miserable, racked with sorrow, but through it all I still know quite certainly that just to be alive is a grand thing.
— Agatha Christie

Do not let your grand ambitions stand in the way of small but meaningful accomplishments.
— Bryant H. McGill

Lavish

The lavish presentation appeals to me, and I've got to convince the others.
— Freddie Mercury

Be always lavish of your caresses, and sparing in your corrections.
— William Cavendish

Legendary

The most successful people I've worked with, like the Rolling Stones - people of a different, kind of legendary caliber - have such great, warm energy.
— Christina Aguilera

The Force is strong with this one.
— Darth Vader

To me a lush carpet of pine needles
or spongy grass is more welcome
than the most luxurious Persian rug.
— Helen Keller

When I go to the shore, I take
along the poems of Pablo Neruda. I
suppose it's because the poems are
simultaneously lush and ripe and
kind of lazy, yet throbbing with life -
like summer itself.
— Tom Robbins

Lush

Habit converts luxurious enjoyments
into dull and daily necessities.
— Aldous Huxley

One of the few luxuries left is travel.
And the aspect of travel that is luxurious is not the movement, but the
being there.
— Andre Balazs

Luxurious

We should be too big to take
offense and too noble to give it.
— Abraham Lincoln

To be really great in little things,
to be truly noble and heroic in the
insipid details of everyday life, is
a virtue so rare as to be worthy
of canonization.
— Harriet Beecher Stowe

Noble

Opulent

Utility is when you have one telephone, luxury is when you have two, opulence is when you have three - and paradise is when you have none.
— Doug Larson

Human prosperity never rests but always craves more, till blown up with pride it totters and falls. From the opulent mansions pointed at by all passersby none warns it away, none cries, 'Let no more riches enter!'
— Aeschylus

Outstanding

Self-denial and self-discipline, however, will be recognized as the outstanding qualities of a good soldier.
— William Lyon Mackenzie King

The origin of life is one of the great outstanding mysteries of science.
— Paul Davies

Posh

I'm not posh or common,
I'm in between.
— Martin Freeman

Cambridge was a joy. Tediously. People reading books in a posh place. It was my fantasy.
— Zadie Smith

Preeminent

The goal of this Nation, I so strongly believe, is to be a preeminent world power. We have to understand what comes with that: The responsibility to be strong.
— Jeff Sessions

Deterrence itself is not a preeminent value; the primary values are safety and morality.
— Herman Kahn

One is taught by experience to put
a premium on those few people who
can appreciate you for what you are.
— Gail Godwin

There is little premium in poetry in
a world that thinks of Pound and
Whitman as a weight and a sam-
pler, not an Ezra, a Walt, a thing of
beauty, a joy forever.
— Anna Quindlen

Premium

Films do seem prestigious and
glamorous, but when you create
something, you want people to see
it. TV still reaches so many more
people; it still really appeals to me.
— Chris Lilley

My only advice is to try to get
the job that's most like the job you
want, rather than the one that's
more prestigious. Always try to be
the talent.
— Ezra Klein

Prestigious

Detailed - Funny

Years ago, I thought up the name
Queen. It's just a name. But it's regal,
obviously, and sounds splendid.
— Freddie Mercury

Every time I see a cardinal, I know my
grandmother is with me. This regal,
red bird was Grandma's favorite.
— Kris Carr

Regal

Selective

I'm a selective pack rat. There's some things I have no problem getting rid of and others I hold onto dearly.
— Will Ferrell

We as Americans and as humans have very selective hearing and very selective memory. We only hear what we want to hear and disregard the rest.
— Frank Luntz

Sophisticated

We are not angels; we are merely sophisticated apes.
— Vilayanur S. Ramachandran

The American public's a lot more sophisticated than we all give them credit for.
— Joe Biden

Stately

A fly, Sir, may sting a stately horse and make him wince; but, one is but an insect, and the other is a horse still.
— Samuel Johnson

There is no more reason to believe that man descended from some inferior animal than there is to believe that a stately mansion has descended from a small cottage.
— William Jennings Bryan

You can't go around hoping that most people have sterling moral characters. The most you can hope for is that people will pretend that they do.
— Fran Lebowitz

Sterling

I know that all cops are not sterling characters. But you have to have someone to root for. I balance it with rotten cops who will take a bribe, who will beat somebody up.
— Evan Hunter

Of all the noises known to man, opera is the most expensive.
— Moliere

Swanky

But I think theatre in a repressive society is an immensely exciting event and theatre in a luxurious old, affluent old society like ours is an entertaining event.
— Janet Suzman

Who could deny that privacy is a jewel? It has always been the mark of privilege, the distinguishing feature of a truly urbane culture.
— Phyllis McGinley

Urbane

The proud make every man their adversary by pitting their intellects, opinions, works, wealth, talents, or any other worldly measuring device against others.
— Ezra Taft Benson

Worldly

You must not forget that you have been given worldly means to use and employ against human arrogance and wrong.
— Knute Nelson

Nothing is sadder than having worldly standards without worldly means.
— Van Wyck Brooks

Emotional

Dramatic

A good many dramatic situations
begin with screaming.
— Jane Fonda

Life can be dramatic and funny all
in the same day.
— Jennifer Aniston

Fanatical

Fanaticism consists of redoubling
your effort when you have forgotten
your aim.
— George Santayana

It is not possible to unknow what
you do know - the result of that
is fanaticism.
— Lionel Blue

Feisty

I love Tinkerbell because she's
feisty and about it.
— Kidada Jones

It's the good girls who keep diaries;
the bad girls never have the time.
— Tallulah Bankhead

Fiery

Never let go of that fiery sadness
called desire.
— Patti Smith

We can only win by giving everything and being ready to defeat the
adversary with fiery aggression.
— Jurgen Klinsmann

When I'm inspired, I get excited
because I can't wait to see what I'll
come up with next.
— Dolly Parton

Hot-blooded

When angry, count to four; when
very angry, swear.
— Mark Twain

Great wisdom is generous; petty
wisdom is contentious. Great
speech is impassioned, small
speech cantankerous.
— Zhuangzi

Impassioned

My mode of presentation is short-
form video - basically I create fast
cut, impassioned 'idea explainers'
that explode with enthusiasm and
intensity as they distill how technology is expanding our sphere
of possibility.
— Jason Silva

Youth is impulsive.
— Chief Seattle

Impulsive

Sometimes I don't know what I want
to do from one day to the next. I can't
enjoy anything premeditated; I just
do it as I feel it. But whatever I do is
motivated by honesty.
— Sharon Tate

I'm going to have my moody times.
— Lucinda Williams

Moody

They say it is better to be poor and
happy than rich and miserable, but
how about a compromise like mod-
erately rich and just moody?
— Princess Diana

Passionate
(see page 379)

Every step toward the goal of justice requires sacrifice, suffering, and struggle; the tireless exertions and passionate concern of dedicated individuals.
— Martin Luther King, Jr.

Nothing is as important as passion. No matter what you want to do with your life, be passionate.
— Jon Bon Jovi

Romantic

A tramp, a gentleman, a poet, a dreamer, a lonely fellow, always hopeful of romance and adventure.
— Charlie Chaplin

There is no charm equal to tenderness of heart.
— Jane Austen

Roused

Roused by the lash of his own stubborn tail our lion now will foreign foes assail.
— John Dryden

It is wonderful what strength of purpose and boldness and energy of will are roused by the assurance that we are doing our duty.
— Walter Scott

Stirring

It is easier to lead men to combat, stirring up their passion, than to restrain them and direct them toward the patient labors of peace.
— Andre Gide

Just keep stirring the pot, you never know what will come up.
— Lee Atwater

There never was any heart truly
great and generous, that was not
also tender and compassionate.
— Robert Frost

Love is an act of endless forgive-
ness, a tender look which becomes
a habit.
— Peter Ustinov

Tender

Soul music is about longevity and
reaching and touching people on
a human level - and that's never
going to get lost.
— Jill Scott

Touching

Well, there's nothing more touching than putting a smile on a kid's
face when you can.
— Emma Roberts

Empowering

Courageous
(see page 123)

The most courageous act is still to think for yourself. Aloud.
— Coco Chanel

He who is not courageous enough to take risks will accomplish nothing in life.
— Muhammad Ali

Positive
(see page 389)

Once you replace negative thoughts with positive ones, you'll start having positive results.
— Willie Nelson

Positive anything is better than negative nothing.
— Elbert Hubbard

Enchanting

Bewitching

Laughter is day, and sobriety is night; a smile is the twilight that hovers gently between both, more bewitching than either.
— Henry Ward Beecher

The wine urges me on, the bewitching wine, which sets even a wise man to singing and to laughing gently, and rouses him up to dance and brings forth words which were better unspoken.
— Homer

Delightful

Truth is so rare that it is delightful to tell it.
— Emily Dickinson

Solitude is painful when one is young, but delightful when one is more mature.
— Albert Einstein

Dreamy

Throw your dreams into space like a kite, and you do not know what it will bring back, a new life, a new friend, a new love, a new country.
— Anais Nin

There are those who look at things the way they are, and ask why. I dream of things that never were, and ask why not?
— Robert Kennedy

Elfin

There is in life an element of elfin coincidence which people reckoning on the prosaic may perpetually miss.
— GK Chesterton

I wouldn't say I was a queen. Maybe a little elf.
— Parker Posey

New York is a fabled city, a fabulous city.
— Italo Calvino

We are like Tolstoy's fabled beggar
who spent his life sitting on a pot of
gold, begging for pennies from every
passerby, unaware that his fortune
was right under him the whole time.
— Elizabeth Gilbert

Fabled

It will be found, in fact, that the
ingenious are always fanciful, and
the truly imaginative never otherwise than analytic.
— Edgar Allan Poe

Knowledge must come through
action; you can have no test, which
is not fanciful; save by trial.
— Sophocles

Fanciful

Stuff your eyes with wonder,
live as if you'd drop dead in ten
seconds. See the world. It's more
fantastic than any dream made or
paid for in factories.
— Ray Bradbury

Fantastic

Poetry, even when apparently
most fantastic, is always a revolt
against artifice, a revolt, in a
sense, against actuality.
— James Joyce

Detailed - Funny

Imaginary

It is a queer thing, but imaginary troubles are harder to bear than actual ones.
— Dorothea Dix

For various reasons, writers retreat into an imaginary world because they find ordinary life rather difficult or boring or both.
— Christopher Koch

Magical

I've always started a movie with a song in my heart, and even when I'm a little unclear about it, something magical happens and it comes into focus in a way that I'm feeling good about.
— Nicolas Cage

The magical, supernatural force that is with us every second is time. We can't even comprehend it. It's such an illusion, it's such a strange thing.
— Anthony Hopkins

Majestic

The centuries-old history and culture of India, majestic architectural monuments and museums of Delhi, Agra and Mumbai have a unique attractive force.
— Vladimir Putin

For sheer majestic geography and sublime scale, nothing beats Alaska and the Yukon. For culture, Japan. And for all-around affection, Australia.
— Sam Abell

There's something about the sound of a train that's very romantic and nostalgic and hopeful.
— Paul Simon

I think the American West really attracts me because it's romantic. The desert, the empty space, the drama.
— Ang Lee

Romantic

Every daring attempt to make a great change in existing conditions, every lofty vision of new possibilities for the human race, has been labeled utopian.
— Emma Goldman

Perhaps I seek certain utopian things, space for human honor and respect, landscapes not yet offended, planets that do not exist yet, dreamed landscapes.
— Werner Herzog

Utopian

Detailed - Funny

Ethereal

Divine

I think the divine is like a huge smile that breaks somewhere in the sea within you, and gradually comes up again.
— John O'Donohue

It is the most divine pleasure to exact the revenge of the brutalized child that resides within.
— Margaret Cho

Exquisite

Words have no power to impress the mind without the exquisite horror of their reality.
— Edgar Allan Poe

I want to lead the Victorian life, surrounded by exquisite clutter.
— Freddie Mercury

Heavenly

Inspiring music may fill the soul with heavenly thoughts, move one to righteous action, or speak peace to the soul.
— Ezra Taft Benson

Wisdom is that apprehension of heavenly things to which the spirit rises through love.
— Honore de Balzac

Holy

Never lose a holy curiosity.
— Albert Einstein

Anybody can observe the Sabbath, but making it holy surely takes the rest of the week.
— Alice Walker

One may not regard the world as
a sort of metaphysical brothel for
emotions.
— Arthur Koestler

Chicago has a strange metaphysical
elegance of death about it.
— Claes Oldenburg

Metaphysical

Music is very nebulous, and you
can conjure up a lot of moods
with music. But lyrics - they're a
lot more tangible. They're much
more specific.
— Sarah McLachlan

I don't want to get hung up on
what 'people,' that nebulous mass,
think about me. That's the way to
unhappiness, I think.
— Monica Ali

Nebulous

Antarctica is otherworldly, like
nothing I've ever seen before. Stark,
cold, beautiful desolation.
— Mark Hoppus

I have long observed that the act of
writing is viewed, by some, as an
elite and otherworldly act, all the
more so if a person isn't paid for
what she writes.
— Joyce Maynard

Otherworldly

We are not human beings having a
spiritual experience. We are spiritual
beings having a human experience.
— Pierre Teilhard de Chardin

Our scientific power has outrun our
spiritual power. We have guided mis-
siles and misguided men.
— Martin Luther King, Jr.

Spiritual

Detailed - Funny

Sublime

Lives of great men all remind us,
we can make our lives sublime, and,
departing, leave behind us, foot-
prints on the sands of time.
— Henry Wadsworth Longfellow

There is only one step from the
sublime to the ridiculous.
— Napoleon Bonaparte

Transcendental

Logic is not a body of doctrine, but
a mirror-image of the world. Logic
is transcendental.
— Ludwig Wittgenstein

I've got a transcendental way
of thinking about things. I've
got a galactic self.
— B.O.

Ethereal and Fast

Fast

Accelerated

The past itself, as historical change continues to accelerate, has become the most surreal of subjects, making it possible to see a new beauty in what is vanishing.
— Susan Sontag

When things begin accelerating wildly out of control, sometimes patience is the only answer.
— Douglas Rushkoff

Agile

Scouts have always been surprised by the way I'm able to move at my size. How fast and agile I am.
— Tyson Chandler

Elves are like trees, grounded and focused from the trunk down but graceful and agile on top.
— Orlando Bloom

Breakneck

Have fun in your command. Don't always run at a breakneck pace. Take leave when you've earned it, spend time with your families.
— Colin Powell

I love doing TV. It's such a break-neck pace, you know. It's kiss and go with your leading man... The filming is over before you know their last names.
— Paulette Goddard

Having countries act on a hair trigger - where they can't afford to be second to strike - the potential for a miscalculation or a nuclear war through inadvertence is simply too high.
— Dennis Ross

A quick temper will make a fool of you soon enough.
— Bruce Lee

Hairtrigger

The sixties were characterized by a heady belief in instantaneous solutions.
— Audre Lorde

It's not a 24-hour news cycle, it's a 60-second news cycle now, it's instantaneous.
— Malcolm Turnbull

Instantaneous

Those little nimble musicians of the air, that warble forth their curious ditties, with which nature hath furnished them to the shame of art.
— Izaak Walton

The point is that instead of a monolithic brick of printed content - delivered more or less unchanged to all subscribers - social media offers news that is personalized and nimble.
— Ryan Holmes

Nimble

Wishing to be friends is quick work, but friendship is a slow ripening fruit.
— Aristotle

A quick temper will make a fool of you soon enough.
— Bruce Lee

Quick

Rapid

In times of rapid change, experience
could be your worst enemy.
— J. Paul Getty

Liberty, when it begins to take root,
is a plant of rapid growth.
— George Washington

Urgent

No duty is more urgent than that of
returning thanks.
— James Allen

We live in a time-crunched world,
and just about everything we do
seems to be urgent.
— Joyce Meyer

Flamboyant

Awesome

The moment one gives close attention to any thing, even a blade of grass it becomes a mysterious, awesome, indescribably magnificent world in itself.
— Henry Miller

I woke up and realized life is great and people are awesome and life is worth living.
— Hulk Hogan

Bombastic

A lot of Hollywood films tend to be bloated, bombastic, loud. At the same time, I do like the infrastructure of making a blockbuster; it's like having a big train set.
— David Yates

It is easy to make sweeping allegations, gloss over facts and figures, and makebombastic claims of corruption and mismanagement.
— David Stuart

Camp

I have a theatrical temperament. I'm not interested in the middle road - maybe because everyone's on it. Rationality, reasonableness bewilder me.
— Joan Didion

I'm cautious about using fire. It can become theatrical. I am interested in the heat, not the flames.
— Andy Goldsworthy

A creative man is motivated by the desire to achieve, not by the desire to beat others.
— Ayn Rand

I am drawn to women who are independent and creative, which is problematic because it's a struggle, a competition of careers.
— Marilyn Manson

Creative
(see page 131)

The emotional brain responds to an event more quickly than the thinking brain.
— Daniel Goleman

Humor is emotional chaos remembered in tranquility.
— James Thurber

Emotional
(see page 179)

I like to make the mundane fabulous whenever I can.
— Rufus Wainwright

True intelligence requires fabulous imagination.
— Ian McEwan

Fabulous

The more far out artists, the better.
— Gary Wright

It's like a novelist writing far out things. If it makes a point and makes sense, then people like to read that. But if it's off in left field and goes over the edge, you lose it.
— Johnny Cash

Far out

Detailed - Funny

Gaudy

A lot of people have said I'd have probably done better in my career if I hadn't looked so cheap and gaudy. But I dress to be comfortable for me, and you shouldn't be blamed because you want to look pretty.
— Dolly Parton

Style is the dress of thought; a modest dress, Neat, but not gaudy, will true critics please.
— Samuel Wesley

Groovy

If anything I consider myself non-violent, I'm from the hippy era, peace, love, groovy.
— Rick James

MTV didn't call. I guess I wasn't hip and groovy enough.
— Dan Fogelberg

Jazzy

I think it's my job to make any question interesting by coming up with a jazzy answer, otherwise I hardly deserve the spotlight, right?
— Michelle Tea

Ikea people do not drive flashy cars or stay at luxury hotels.
— Ingvar Kamprad

Nifty

I'm so not stylish by nature, but I've learned to work with what I have.
— Julie Bowen

I understand that most iPhone users want a phone that can do other nifty things, not a general purpose computer that happens to make phone calls.
— Jamais Cascio

I have a theory that if you're
famous more years than you're not
famous, then you get a little nutty.
— Dana Carvey

Life is nutty; anything can happen.
— Paul Shaffer

Nutty

I grew up watching all these crazy
movies, European movies and stuff,
and I guess that I always laughed at
things that were a little more offbeat.
— Louis C. K.

I don't think of myself as offbeat and
weird. As a kid, I saw myself as the
type of guy who would run into a
burning building to save the baby.
— Christian Slater

Offbeat
(see page 367)

Partial culture runs to the ornate;
extreme culture to simplicity.
— Christian Nevell Bovee

If I'm researching something
strange and rococo, I'll go to the
London Library or the British
Library and look it up in books.
— Ben Schott

Rococo

I've always had an innate ability
to dance, but I'm not as spiffy as
those cinema legends like Gene
Kelly and Fred Astaire.
— John Travolta

To me, Cary Grant is probably the
most fashionable man in the history of Hollywood. The guy
was just slick.
— Reid Scott Delicious

Spiffy

Detailed - Funny

Flavorful

Delicious

The air soft as that of Seville in
April, and so fragrant that it was
delicious to breathe it.
— Christopher Columbus

Yet, it is true, poetry is delicious;
the best prose is that which is most
full of poetry.
— Virginia Woolf

Piquant

Taste, which enables us to distinguish all that has a flavor from that
which is insipid.
— Jean Anthelme Brillat-Savarin

The most exciting attractions are
between two opposites that never meet.
— Andy Warhol

Salty

I still have highs and lows; maybe
I don't cry salty tears as much.
— Sarah Silverman

Chocolate is not cheating! After a
salty meal, you need a little bit of
sweet. This is living, not cheating.
— Ali Landry

Savory

Let the stoics say what they please,
we do not eat for the good of living,
but because the meat is savory and
the appetite is keen.
— Ralph Waldo Emerson

Balance is key in cooking - you
want a little acid, a little sweet, a
little savory - the flavors should be
harmonious.
— Gail Simmons

I'm trying to lead a good Christian life, so there ain't too much spicy to tell about me.
— Loretta Lynn

I think Nina Simone has had an amazing journey. She was spicy and she had attitude and she didn't care...
— Nia Long

Spicy

The roots of education are bitter, but the fruit is sweet.
— Aristotle

I write with humour about sadness, to introduce an element of sweet to the sour, a bit like Turkish food.
— Elif Safak

Sweet

Zest is the secret of all beauty. There is no beauty that is attractive without zest.
— Christian Dior

True happiness comes from the joy of deeds well done, the zest of creating things new.
— Antoine de Saint-Exupery

Zesty

Detailed - Funny

Free

Bohemian

I'm a girl from a good family who was very well brought up. One day I turned my back on it all and became a bohemian.
— Brigitte Bardot

I used to think then that I was bohemian, but I know now that I am not. I prefer order and precision to untidiness and looseness.
— Conrad Veidt

Boundless

The world of reality has its limits; the world of imagination is boundless.
— Jean-Jacques Rousseau

Dogs have boundless enthusiasm but no sense of shame. I should have a dog as a life coach.
— Moby

Crazy

A question that sometimes drives me hazy: am I or are the others crazy?
— Albert Einstein

I just had a crazy, wild imagination all my life, and science fiction is the greatest outlet for me.
— Steven Spielberg

Foot-loose

I'm single, footloose and fancy free; I have no responsibilities, no anchors. Work, friendship and self-improvement, that's me.
— Joel Edgerton

Some people are drawn naturally - there are natural guitarists, and there are natural piano players, and I think guitar implies travel, a sort of foot-loose gypsy existence. You grab your bag and you go to the next town.
— Hugh Laurie

I am no bird, and no net ensnares
me; I am a free human being with an
independent will.
— Charlotte Bronte

Hope is independent of the appara-
tus of logic.
— Norman Cousins

Independent

It's mind-altering when you slip
into someone else's shoes. That's
psychedelic, man.
— Bryan Cranston

I always saw Michael Gambon
wearing madly psychedelic socks...
— Daniel Radcliffe

Psychedelic

Love to faults is always blind,
always is to joy inclined. Law-
less, winged, and unconfined, and
breaks all chains from every mind.
— William Shakespeare

On with the dance; let joy be
unconfined is my motto, whether
there's any dance to dance or any
joy to unconfined.
— Mark Twain.

Unconfined

There's a tremendous freedom that
comes from being unfettered by
your own familiar culture, and by
seeing the world from a different
point of view.
— Kim Edwards

The scientists often have more
unfettered imaginations than current philosophers do.
— Robert Nozick

Unfettered

Detailed - Funny

Wandering

If a man's wit be wandering, let him study the mathematics.
— Francis Bacon

I've always found a cure for the blues is wandering into something unknown, and resting there, before coming back to whatever weight you were carrying.
— Diane Sawyer

Wild

You were once wild here. Don't let them tame you.
— Isadora Duncan

A man without ethics is a wild beast loosed upon this world.
— Albert Camus

Free and Funny

Funny

Absurd

It is absurd to divide people into good and bad. People are either charming or tedious.
— Oscar Wilde

The fact that an opinion has been widely held is no evidence whatever that it is not utterly absurd.
— Bertrand Russell

Amusing

At first, I only laughed at myself. Then I noticed that life itself is amusing. I've been in a generally good mood ever since.
— Marilyn vos Savant

I enjoyed the courtroom as just another stage but not so amusing as Broadway.
— Mae West

Confident (see page 109)

All those hours exploring the great outdoors made me more resilient and confident.
— David Suzuki

So confident am I in the intentions, as well as wisdom, of the government, that I shall always be satisfied that what is not done, either cannot, or ought not to be done.
— Thomas Jefferson

Contagious

A healthy attitude is contagious, but don't wait to catch it from others. Be a carrier.
— Tom Stoppard

Freedom is the most contagious virus known to man.
— Hubert H. Humphrey

So, deadpan I think just means not
acknowledging for one second that
you think that this is funny and clever.
— Patrick Warburton

Though the clown is often deadpan,
he is a connoisseur of laughter.
— Mel Gussow

Deadpan

This shirt is dry clean only. Which
means... it's dirty.
— Mitch Hedberg

A sincere diplomat is like dry water
or wooden iron.
— Joseph Stalin

Dry

I know my life is full of awkward
pauses, and I think it's hilarious.
— Josh Hutcherson

My favorite kind of humor is basically, if it was happening to you, it
wouldn't be funny, but to observe it,
it's hilarious.
— Bill Burr

Hilarious

I can imagine no more comfortable
frame of mind for the conduct of life
than a humorous resignation.
— W. Somerset Maugham

You know, my main reaction to this
money thing is that it's humorous,
all the attention to it, because it's
hardly the most insightful or valuable thing that's happened to me.
— Steve Jobs

Humorous

Detailed - Funny

Infectious

The media has become more forceful, has begun to recognize its traditional historic role and act on it, and truth is infectious.
— Ron Suskind

Love is infectious and the greatest healing energy.
— Sai Baba

Ironic

It is an ironic habit of human beings to run faster when we have lost our way.
— Rollo May

There's nothing more ironic or contradictory than life itself.
— Robert De Niro

Irreverent

Original thought, original artistic expression is by its very nature questioning, irreverent, iconoclastic.
— Salman Rushdie

I hate the irreverent rabble and keep them far from me.
— Horace

Ludicrous

The loss of young first love is so painful that it borders on the ludicrous.
— Maya Angelou

I could feel his muscle tissues collapse under my force. It's ludicrous these mortals even attempt to enter my realm.
— Mike Tyson

I've always chosen incredibly different roles and things that are quite
offbeat. That way you're not limited.
— Anna Friel

You can time a part perfectly and
play it badly. And some people
have very individual offbeat timing,
which is their own. It works simply
because they are who they are.
— Alan Bates

Offbeat
(see page 367)

(see page 367)

Every author, however modest, keeps
a most outrageous vanity chained
like a madman in the padded cell of
his breast.
— Logan Pearsall Smith

One can be absolutely truthful and
sincere even though admittedly the
most outrageous liar. Fiction and
invention are of the very fabric of life.
— Henry Miller

Outrageous

It is requisite for the relaxation of the
mind that we make use, from time to
time, of playful deeds and jokes.
— Thomas Aquinas

We all want to be a little glamorous,
a little playful and a little mischievous at times.
— Jason Wu

Playful

Detailed - Funny

Ridiculous

I have never made but one prayer to God, a very short one: 'O Lord make my enemies ridiculous.' And God granted it.
— Voltaire

It is ridiculous to set a detective story in New York City. New York City is itself a detective story.
— Agatha Christie

Sarcastic

Why do we laugh at such terrible things? Because comedy is often the sarcastic realization of inescapable tragedy.
— Bryant H. McGill

For me and my entire generation, we took on this kind of sarcastic, ironic, snarkiness because it seemed the most extreme reaction to the earnestness of hippies.
— Chuck Palahniuk

Silly

Mix a little foolishness with your serious plans. It is lovely to be silly at the right moment.
— Horace

I've been bitten by a python. Not a very big one. I was being silly, saying: 'Oh, it's not poisonous...' Then, wallop!
— David Attenborough

People who can't be witty exert themselves to be devout and affectionate.
— George Eliot

One cannot be always laughing at a
man without now and then stumbling
on something witty.
— Jane Austen

Witty

There are no straight backs, no
symmetrical faces, many wry noses,
and no even legs. We are a crooked
and perverse generation.
— William Osler

Wry

James Bond is quite serious about
his drinks and clothing and ciga-
rettes and food and all that sort
of thing. There is nothing wry or
amused about James Bond.
— Ken Follet

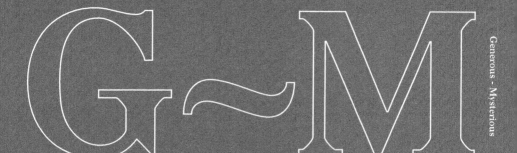

G~M

Generous - Mysterious

Generous

Altruistic

Elephants have the largest brains of any mammal on the face of the Earth. They are creative, altruistic, and kind.
— Ingrid Newkirk

The great majority of people are calm, resourceful, altruistic or even beyond altruistic, as they risk themselves for others. We improvise the conditions of survival beautifully.
— Rebecca Solnit

Benevolent

But friendship is precious, not only in the shade, but in the sunshine of life, and thanks to a benevolent arrangement the greater part of life is sunshine.
— Thomas Jefferson

We always like to keep our children in a kind of bubble and censor the bad news about the world. We like to tell them the world is full of benevolent, nice people.
— Kazuo Ishiguro

Compassionate (see page 103)

There never was any heart truly great and generous, that was not also tender and compassionate.
— Robert Frost

If a photographer cares about the people before the lens and is compassionate, much is given.
— Eve Arnold

Just being hired by a great director
is complimentary.
— Tom Skerritt

I often wish that so many people,
who just work normal jobs, could
get a pat on the back as much as I
do, because it's very complimentary.
— Michael Ealy

Complimentary

For it is in giving that we receive.
— Francis of Assisi

Happiness... consists in giving,
and in serving others.
— Henry Drummond

Giving

I am the most helpful and open up
doors for everyone and I like to share.
— Arnold Schwarzenegger

I say you don't need religion, or
political ideology, to understand
human nature. Science reveals that
human nature is greedy and selfish,
altruistic and helpful.
— Michael Shermer

Helpful

With reasonable men, I will reason;
with humane men I will plead; but
to tyrants I will give no quarter, nor
waste arguments where they will
certainly be lost.
— William Lloyd Garrison

What do you regard as most
humane? To spare someone shame.
— Friedrich Nietzsche

Humane

Positive
(see page 389)

Few things in the world are more powerful than a positive push. A smile. A world of optimism and hope. A 'you can do it' when things are tough.
— Richard M. DeVos

You can't make positive choices for the rest of your life without an environment that makes those choices easy, natural, and enjoyable.
— Deepak Chopra

Willing

If you are not willing to risk the unusual, you will have to settle for the ordinary.
— Jim Rohn

If you're not willing to work hard, let someone else do it. I'd rather be with someone who does a horrible job, but gives 110% than with someone who does a good job and gives 60%.
— Will Smith

Happy

Auspicious

One should try to take inspirations from great people and engage one-self in auspicious deeds.
— Sam Veda

November is auspicious in so many parts of the country: the rice harvest is already in, the weather starts to cool, and the festive glow which precedes Christmas has began to brighten the landscape.
— F. Sionil Jose

Bouncy

It's so often that I read for the bouncy, sunny girl men fall in love with who will solve all the romantic problems in the narrative.
— Sarah Gadon

A lively understandable spirit once entertained you. It will come again. Be still. Wait.
— Theodore Roethke

Cheerful

Wondrous is the strength of cheerfulness, and its power of endurance - the cheerful man will do more in the same time, will do it; better, will preserve it longer, than the sad or sullen.
— Thomas Carlyle

The person who can be only serious or only cheerful, is but half a man.
— Leigh Hunt

You can be childlike without being childish. A child always wants to have fun. Ask yourself, 'Am I having fun?'
— Christopher Meloni

It is the childlike mind that finds the kingdom.
— Charles Fillmore

Childlike

I grew up in Minnesota and everyone is so nice there. It is like Fargo. Everyone's so chipper and you make friends just grocery shopping. We kill each other with kindness.
— Seann William Scott

To keep the heart unwrinkled, to be hopeful, kindly, cheerful, reverent that is to triumph over old age.
— Amos Bronson Alcott

Chipper

Happiness consists not in having much, but in being content with little.
— Marguerite Gardiner

Life is so impermanent that it's not about somebody else or things around me, it's about knowing you are completely alone in this world and being content inside.
— K. D. Lang

Content

Delightful

No occupation is so delightful to me as the culture of the earth, and no culture comparable to that of the garden.
— Thomas Jefferson

I suppose society is wonderfully delightful. To be in it is merely a bore. But to be out of it is simply a tragedy.
— Oscar Wilde

Delirious

I'm delirious with joy. It proves that if you confront the universe with good intentions in your heart, it will reflect that and reward your intent. Usually.
— J. Michael Straczynski

Frazzled and delirious, as I've just finished a new book of stories. I feel like Moses staggering down the mountainside with the tablets of stone.
— Kevin Barry

Effervescent

Playwrights have texts, composers have scores, painters and sculptors have the residue of those activities, and dance is traditionally an ephemeral, effervescent, here-today-gone-tomorrow kind of thing.
— Twyla Tharp

There are things that haunt us our entire lives; we are unable to let them go. The good times seem almost effervescent and dreamlike in comparison with the times that didn't go so well.
— Henry Rollins

I was elated, ecstatic, and
extremely surprised that we
were successful.
— Neil Armstrong

Never elated when someone's
oppressed, never dejected when
another one's blessed.
— Alexander Pope

Elated

No virtue is safe that is not
enthusiastic.
— John Robert Seeley

I'm in an agreeable state: busy,
enthusiastic, curious.
— Isabelle Adjani

Enthusiastic

I believe that education is all about
being excited about something. Seeing passion and enthusiasm helps
push an educational message.
— Steve Irwin

The more excited the rooster gets,
the higher his voice goes. He's got
a little bit of a Barney Fife quality
to him.
— Jeff Foxworthy

Excited

I tend to think of action movies as
exuberant morality plays in which
good triumphs over evil.
— Sylvester Stallone

Designers have always shown outland-
ish and exuberant clothes, but that
hasn't always translated to the streets.
— Jason Wu

Exuberant

Giddy

If anybody says he can think about quantum physics without getting giddy, that only shows he has not understood the first thing about them.
— Niels Bohr

He that is giddy thinks the world turns round.
— William Shakespeare

Jolly

Well, my deliberate opinion is - it's a jolly strange world.
— Arnold Bennett

There's nothing like a jolly good disaster to get people to start doing something.
— Prince Charles

Joyous

When you are joyous, look deep into your heart and you shall find it is only that which has given you sorrow that is giving you joy.
— Khalil Gibran

A laugh, to be joyous, must flow from a joyous heart, for without kindness, there can be no true joy.
— Thomas Carlyle

Optimistic (see page 375)

I would feel more optimistic about a bright future for man if he spent less time proving that he can outwit nature and more time tasting her sweetness and respecting her seniority.
— E. B. White

There is a sense that things, if you keep positive and optimistic about what can be done, do work out.
— Hillary Clinton

We sold out all over the world,
and every night I looked out into
the fans and those front rows that
you're talking about, the tears,
the honesty, the inability to not be
completely overjoyed because they
felt accepted.
— Lady Gaga

Overjoyed

Remember, no human condition is
ever permanent. Then you will not
be overjoyed in good fortune nor
too scornful in misfortune.
— Socrates

I obviously take a lot of pride
in what I do on the football field,
because that has the ability to
influence a lot of people. That
puts smiles on people's faces.
That gives people a pep in their
step on Monday morning when
they go back to work.
— Drew Brees

Peppy

A man is free to go up as high as
he can reach up to; but I, with all
my style and pep, can't get a man
my equal because a girl is always
judged by her mother.
— Anzia Yezierska

One's age should be tranquil,
as childhood should be playful.
— Thomas Arnold

Playful

I envy guys who are consistently
able to maintain a playful, optimistic perspective on things.
— Eric Dane

Positive
(see page 389)

Positive thinking will let you do everything better than negative thinking will.
— Zig Ziglar

If you have a positive attitude and constantly strive to give your best effort, eventually you will overcome your immediate problems and find you are ready for greater challenges.
— Pat Riley

Smiling

I've had to learn to fight all my life - got to learn to keep smiling. If you smile things will work out.
— Serena Williams

When I look out at the people and they look at me and they're smiling, then I know that I'm loved.
— Etta James

Upbeat

Being upbeat is the key to life.
— David Frost

So even though I consider myself a fairly upbeat person, energetic and things like that, I never do very well on happiness tests.
— Barbara Ehrenreich

Vibrant
(see page 499)

As children, our imaginations are vibrant, and our hearts are open.
— Yehuda Berg

What is needed in the theater, in fact for all our art forms, is a vibrant critical tradition.
— F. Sionil Jose

Caves are whimsical things, and
geology on a local scale is random
and unpredictable.
— William Stone

For me it was really important to
get the essence out of the music
for the story and not, sort of, press
the music into the service of the
whimsical telling of it.
— Graeme Murphy

Whimsical

If you're walking down the right path
and you're willing to keep walking,
eventually you'll make progress.
— Barack Obama

We must be willing to let go of the
life we have planned, so as to have
the life that is waiting for us.
— E. M. Forster

Willing

The brain is a wonderful organ;
it starts working the moment you
get up in the morning and does not
stop until you get into the office.
— Robert Frost

How wonderful it is that nobody
need wait a single moment before
starting to improve the world.
— Anne Frank

Wonderful

Brownie's Guide to Expertly Defined Ideas

Heritage

Ancient

Myths can't be translated as they did in their ancient soil. We can only find our own meaning in our own time.
— Margaret Atwood

Let others praise ancient times; I am glad I was born in these.
— Ovid

Enduring

I love love, and I love life. I love. I just love. It's just great. It's the most enduring element we have is love.
— Gary Busey

The lesson I have thoroughly learnt, and wish to pass on to others, is to know the enduring happiness that the love of a garden gives.
— Gertrude Jekyll

Experienced

For me, there are two types of people: the young and the experienced.
— A. P. J. Abdul Kalam

Human vocabulary is still not capable, and probably never will be, of knowing, recognizing, and communicating everything that can be humanly experienced and felt.
— Jose Saramago

Grounded

When adversity strikes, that's when you have to be the most calm. Take a step back, stay strong, stay grounded, and press on.
— LL Cool J

There was a point after the whole intensity of the Clash finally subsided when I just found that painting grounded me in a way that music didn't.
— Paul Simon

Waiting is painful. Forgetting is painful. But not knowing which to do is the worse kind of suffering.
— Paulo Coelho

A cynical young person is almost the saddest sight to see, because it means that he or she has gone from knowing nothing to believing nothing.
— Maya Angelou

Knowing

You can't just beat a team; you have to leave a lasting impression in their minds so they never want to see you again.
— Mia Hamm

In order to acquire a growing and lasting respect in society, it is a good thing, if you possess great talent, to give, early in your youth, a very hard kick to the right shin of the society that you love. After that, be a snob.
— Salvador Dali

Lasting

There's a part of you that always remains a child, no matter how mature you get, how sophisticated or weary.
— Barbra Streisand

The rate at which a person can mature is directly proportional to the embarrassment he can tolerate.
— Douglas Engelbart

Mature

Perennial

I am very much a person who appreciates perennial things. Things like a Lacoste shirt, a Clarks desert boot, Persol sunglasses and Vans shoes that have been the same forever.
— Roman Coppola

Pleasure is a shadow, wealth is vanity, and power a pageant; but knowledge is ecstatic in enjoyment, perennial in frame, unlimited in space and indefinite in duration.
— DeWitt Clinton

Perpetual

Revolution is not something fixed in ideology, nor is it something fashioned to a particular decade. It is a perpetual process embedded in the human spirit.
— Abbie Hoffman

I were better to be eaten to death with a rust than to be scoured to nothing with perpetual motion.
— William Shakespeare

Responsible

Perhaps it is better to be irresponsible and right, than to be responsible and wrong.
— Winston Churchill

One must always be aware, to notice even though the cost of noticing is to become responsible.
— Thylias Moss

I'm a romantic; a sentimental
person thinks things will last,
a romantic person hopes against
hope that they won't.
— F. Scott Fitzgerald

Intellectuals are too
sentimental for me.
— Margaret Anderson

Sentimental

It amazes me sometimes that even
intelligent people will analyze a
situation or make a judgement after
only recognizing the standard or
traditional structure of a piece.
— David Bowie

New York is traditional New York,
you know what I'm saying? It's the
stomping ground of the hustlers
and go-getters.
— Busta Rhymes

Traditional

A wise man can learn more from
a foolish question than a fool can
learn from a wise answer.
— Bruce Lee

It is wise to persuade people to do
things and make them think it was
their own idea.
— Nelson Mandela

Wise

Generous - Mysterious

Heroic

Bold

Be bold. If you're going to make an error, make a doozy, and don't be afraid to hit the ball.
— Billie Jean King

I'm going to make a very bold statement: Hip-hop has done more than any leader, politician, or anyone to improve race relations.
— Jay-Z

Brave

I beg you take courage; the brave soul can mend even disaster.
— Catherine the Great

I learned that courage was not the absence of fear, but the triumph over it. The brave man is not he who does not feel afraid, but he who conquers that fear.
— Nelson Mandela

Confident (see page 109)

Confidence comes from within and as long as you are putting forth a respectable effort to take good care of yourself, you should feel confident about that path.
— Stacy Keibler

I think it's the mark of a great player to be confident in tough situations.
— John McEnroe

Courageous

The most courageous act is still to think for yourself. Aloud.
— Coco Chanel

For us, someone who is willing to step forward and help is much more courageous than someone who is merely fulfilling the role.
— Margaret J. Wheatley

Life is either a daring adventure,
or nothing.
— Helen Keller

My life has been long, and believing
that life loves the liver of it, I have
dared to try many things, sometimes trembling, but daring still.
— Maya Angelou

Daring

When someone is iconic it means
they have established a certain kind
of legacy possibly, and I think it
does come with time.
— Diana Ross

Any time you change something
classic or iconic, you're going to
have some part of the fan base up
in arms.
— Jim Lee

Iconic

Gratitude is the sign of noble souls.
— Aesop

To be really great in little things,
to be truly noble and heroic in the
insipid details of everyday life, is a
virtue so rare as to be worthy
of canonization.
— Harriet Beecher Stowe

Noble

He who believes is strong; he who
doubts is weak. Strong convictions
precede great actions.
— Louisa May Alcott

Truth is strong, and sometime or
other will prevail.
— Mary Astell

Strong
(see page 449)

Unafraid

I feel myself becoming the fearless
person I have dreamt of being. Have
I arrived? No. But I'm constantly
evolving and challenging myself to
be unafraid to make mistakes.
— Janelle Monae

The flower has opened, has been in
the sun and is unafraid. I'm taking
more chances; I'm bold and proud.
— Paula Cole

2 OUTTA 3
AIN'T BAD !

Heroic and Honest

Honest

Accountable

Human beings should be held accountable. Leave God alone. He has enough problems.
— Elie Wiesel

You cannot hold a child accountable to the same standards that you hold an adult accountable to.
— Alan Ball

Authentic
(see page 31)

Without culture, and the relative freedom it implies, society, even when perfect, is but a jungle. This is why any authentic creation is a gift to the future.
— Albert Camus

The authentic self is the soul made visible.
— Sarah Ban Breathnach

Bonafide

Don't learn to do, but learn in doing. Let your falls not be on a prepared ground, but let them be bona fide falls in the rough and tumble of the world.
— Samuel Butler

One man alone can be pretty dumb sometimes, but for real bona fide stupidity, there ain't nothin' can beat teamwork.
— Edward Abbey

If I write a book where all I've ever experienced is success, people won't take a positive lesson from it. In being candid, I have to own up to my own failures, both in my marriage and in my work environment.
— Sonia Sotomayor

I have always felt that a woman has the right to treat the subject of her age with ambiguity until, perhaps, she passes into the realm of over ninety. Then it is better she be candid with herself and with the world.
— Carl Sandburg

Candid

We might all place ourselves in one of two ranks the women who do something, and the women who do nothing; the first being of course the only creditable place to occupy.
— Lucy Larcom

I assume that - because you can get degrees in journalism from very reputable universities - I assume that people can be trained to be journalists.
— William Gibson

Creditable

People who are high on openness to experience just crave novelty, variety, diversity, new ideas, travel. People low on it like things that are familiar, that are safe and dependable.
— Jonathan Haidt

There's nothing like a really loyal, dependable, good friend. Nothing.
— Jennifer Aniston

Dependable

Earnest

Deeply earnest and thoughtful people stand on shaky footing with the public.
— Johann Wolfgang von Goethe

The squirrel that you kill in jest, dies in earnest.
— Henry David Thoreau

Equitable

Apart from values and ethics which I have tried to live by, the legacy I would like to leave behind is a very simple one - that I have always stood up for what I consider to be the right thing, and I have tried to be as fair and equitable as I could be.
— Ratan Tata

Inclusive, good-quality education is a foundation for dynamic and equitable societies.
— Desmond Tutu

Ethical

The industrial revolution has tended to produce everywhere great urban masses that seem to be increasingly careless of ethical standards.
— Irving Babbitt

Ethical decisions ensure that everyone's best interests are protected. When in doubt, don't.
— Harvey Mackay

Faithful

Be faithful in small things because it is in them that your strength lies.
— Mother Teresa

There are three faithful friends - an old wife, an old dog, and ready money.
— Benjamin Franklin

The tragedy of bold, forthright,
industrious people is that they act so
continuously without much thinking,
that it becomes dry and empty.
— Brenda Ueland

It is a sure sign of trouble when
things can no longer be called by
their right names and described
in plain, forthright speech.
— Christopher Lasch

Forthright

Genuine poetry can communicate
before it is understood.
— T. S. Eliot

The more one does and sees and
feels, the more one is able to do,
and the more genuine may be
one's appreciation of fundamental
things like home, and love, and
understanding companionship.
— Amelia Earhart

Genuine

A life spent making mistakes is not
only more honorable, but more useful than a life spent doing nothing.
— George Bernard Shaw

One of the common failings among
honorable people is a failure to
appreciate how thoroughly dishonorable some other people can be, and
how dangerous it is to trust them.
— Thomas Sowell

Honorable

Imperfect

I don't want to be perfect, but I do want to be a role model.
— Miley Cyrus

Existence really is an imperfect tense that never becomes a present.
— Friedrich Nietzsche

Just

Our greatest happiness does not depend on the condition of life in which chance has placed us, but is always the result of a good conscience, good health, occupation, and freedom in all just pursuits.
— Thomas Jefferson

The demand for equal rights in every vocation of life is just and fair; but, after all, the most vital right is the right to love and be loved.
— Emma Goldman

Moral

Voting is the most precious right of every citizen, and we have a moral obligation to ensure the integrity of our voting process.
— Hillary Clinton

Music is a moral law.
— Plato

Remembering that you are going
to die is the best way I know to
avoid the trap of thinking you have
something to lose. You are already
naked. There is no reason not to follow your heart.
— Steve Jobs

Naked

Facts which at first seem improb-
able will, even on scant explanation,
drop the cloak which has hidden
them and stand forth in naked and
simple beauty.
— Galileo Galilei

A word to the wise ain't necessary - it's
the stupid ones that need the advice.
— Bill Cosby

Necessary

It is not necessary to change. Survival is not mandatory.
— W. Edwards Deming

The challenge for me has first been
to see things as they are, whether a
portrait, a city street, or a bouncing
ball. In a word, I have tried to be
objective.
— Berenice Abbott

Objective

Objective journalism and an opinion
column are about as similar as the
Bible and Playboy magazine.
— Walter Cronkite

Generous - Mysterious

Open

I have always kept an open mind, a flexibility that must go hand in hand with every form of the intelligent search for truth.
— Malcolm X

The most valuable possession you can own is an open heart.
— Carlos Santana

Outspoken

Boxing gave me discipline; a sense of self. It made me more outspoken. It gave me more confidence.
— Sugar Ray Leonard

If you aren't overly effusive or really nicey-nice with the press, you get a reputation for being outspoken or difficult.
— Janeane Garofalo

Overt

Laws undertake to punish only overt acts.
— Charles de Montesquieu

Hibernation is a covert preparation for a more overt action.
— Ralph Ellison

Public

We never really grow up, we only learn how to act in public.
— Bryan White

If I have done the public any service, it is due to my patient thought.
— Isaac Newton

It is health that is real wealth and not
pieces of gold and silver.
— Mahatma Gandhi

Reality is wrong. Dreams are for real.
— Tupac Shakur

Real

The heart is the best reflective
thinker.
— Wendell Phillips

A verbal art like poetry is reflective; it stops to think.
— W. H. Auden

Reflective

Animals are reliable, many full
of love, true in their affections,
predictable in their actions, grateful
and loyal. Difficult standards for
people to live up to.
— Alfred A. Montapert

If only shame were a reliable engine
for behavior modification.
— Ayelet Waldman

Reliable

When resonant harmonies arise
between this vast outer cosmos and the
inner human cosmos, poetry is born.
— Daisaku Ikeda

The sort of thing that I want to do is
to strike a resonant chord of univer-
sality in other people, which is best
done by fiction.
— Joyce Carol Oates

Resonant

Generous - Mysterious

Sincere

One of the most sincere forms of respect is actually listening to what another has to say.
— Bryant H. McGill

The sincere friends of this world are as ship lights in the stormiest of nights.
— Giotto di Bondone

Straight

Good things happen when you get your priorities straight.
— Scott Caan

A smile is a curve that sets everything straight.
— Phyllis Diller

Substantial

Redirect the substantial energy of your frustration and turn it into positive, effective, unstoppable determination.
— Ralph Marston

Substantial progress toward better things can rarely be taken without developing new evils requiring new remedies.
— William Howard Taft

Telling

A memoir is always the most authentic telling of a situation, but a novel gets to different places.
— Emma Donoghue

I think your conversations are indicative of your tastes - even your diction.
— Miguel

The most important role of a leader
is to set a clear direction, be transparent about how to get there and
to stay the course.
— Irene Rosenfeld

I wish that every human life might
be pure transparent freedom.
— Simone de Beauvoir

Transparent

Being taken for granted can be a
compliment. It means that you've
become a comfortable, trusted element in another person's life.
— Joyce Brothers

To be trusted is a greater compliment than being loved.
— George MacDonald

Trusted

To be persuasive we must be believable; to be believable we must be
credible; credible we must be truthful.
— Edward R. Murrow

A man is never more truthful than
when he acknowledges himself a liar.
— Mark Twain

Truthful

There will always be some who
wimp out and second-guess when
the pain hits.
— Nathan Myhrvold

Just because you're upfront with
someone doesn't mean you're an
honest person; you might just be
someone in the passenger seat.
— Brian Celio

Upfront

Generous - Mysterious

Upright

There is only one position for an artist anywhere; and that is upright.
— Dylan Thomas

I think penguins are the most human of all the birds, which may be why people love them. They're cute, they stand upright and they look like they're wearing tuxedos.
— Shia LaBeouf

Human

Accessible
(see page 15)

Everyone likes birds. What wild creature is more accessible to our eyes and ears, as close to us and everyone in the world, as universal as a bird?
— David Attenborough

As a woman, you're not accessible to every world.
— Zaha Hadid

Casual
(see page 65)

I'm a sweats and UGGs girl. Very casual.
— Jennifer Aniston

The true nature of evil is that it is so very casual.
— James St. James

Compassionate
(see page 103)

More compassionate mind, more sense of concern for other's well-being, is source of happiness.
— Dalai Lama

I think having a dog makes you more compassionate.
— Cheyenne Jackson

Emotional
(see page 179)

I took so many bad things as a kid and some people think I don't care about anything. It's just too hard for me to get emotional. I can't cry no more.
— Mike Tyson

Never build your emotional life on the weaknesses of others.
— George Santayana

Fame is empowering.
— Charlie Sheen

It's great being your own boss, but
then, you know, you make your own
mistakes, you know, and you own
them. You know, so it's empowering,
and it's also humbling along the way.
— Ani DiFranco

Empowering
(see page 185)

An honest man is always a child.
— Socrates

Me, I'm dishonest, and you can
always trust a dishonest man to be
dishonest. Honestly, it's the honest
ones you have to watch out for.
— Johnny Depp

Honest
(see page 267)

Don't be humble... you're not that great.
— Golda Meir

At home I am a nice guy: but I don't
want the world to know. Humble
people, I've found, don't get very far.
— Muhammad Ali

Humble
(see page 287)

I have learned that there is more
power in a good strong hug than
in a thousand meaningful words.
— Ann Hood

Empathy is really the opposite
of spiritual meanness. It's the
capacity to understand that every
war is both won and lost. And that
someone else's pain is as meaningful as your own.
— Barbara Kingsolver

Meaningful
(see page 325)

Optimistic
(see page 375)

'Rocky' represents the optimistic side of life, and 'Rambo' represents purgatory.
— Sylvester Stallone

Ultimately, because I'm an artist, I can't ever consider myself a nihilist, so I suppose I'm optimistic.
— Marilyn Manson

Purposeful
(see page 399)

The purpose of art is washing the dust of daily life off our souls.
— Pablo Picasso

Everything in our society is so purposeful. Let's bring joy back to the experience.
— Sarah Blakely

Humble

Courteous

Be peaceful, be courteous, obey the law, respect everyone; but if someone puts his hand on you, send him to the cemetery.
— Malcolm X

Be courteous to all, but intimate with few, and let those few be well tried before you give them your confidence.
— George Washington

Coy

I'm not trying to be sexy. It's just my way of expressing myself when I move around.
— Elvis Presley

Then be not coy, but use your time.
— Robert Herrick

Demure

Truth is a demure lady, much too ladylike to knock you on your head and drag you to her cave.
— William F. Buckley, Jr.

Don't try to be what you're not. If you're nervous, be nervous. If you're shy, be shy. It's cute.
— Adriana Lima

Hushed

I like the evening in India, the one magic moment when the sun balances on the rim of the world, and the hush descends, and ten thousand civil servants drift homeward on a river of bicycles.
— James Cameron

The library, with its Daedalian labyrinth, mysterious hush, and faintly ominous aroma of knowledge, has been replaced by the computer's cheap glow, pesky chirp, and data spillage.
— P. J. O'Rourke

The innocent and the beautiful have
no enemy but time.
— William Butler Yeats

Saints should always be judged guilty
until they are proved innocent.
— George Orwell

Innocent

It's passionately interesting for me
that the things that I learned in a
small town, in a very modest home,
are just the things that I believe
have won the election.
— Margaret Thatcher

Modesty is a learned affectation.
And as soon as life slams the modest person against the wall, that
modesty drops.
— Maya Angelou

Modest

Surfing soothes me. The ocean is so
magnificent, peaceful, and awesome. The rest of the world disap-
pears for me when I'm on a wave.
— Paul Walker

Wars are poor chisels for carving
out peaceful tomorrows.
— Martin Luther King, Jr.

Peaceful

Be polite; write diplomatically; even
in a declaration of war one observes
the rules of politeness.
— Otto von Bismarck

An armed society is a polite society.
Manners are good when one may
have to back up his acts with his life.
— Robert A. Heinlein

Polite

Generous - Mysterious

Reserved
(see page 411)

Ignorance is bold and knowledge reserved.
— Thucydides

Usually the modest person passes for someone reserved, the silent for a sullen person.
— Horace

Respectful

On everything I do I'm always taking someone's money, whether it's a movie studio or a record label. Somebody's paying for it, and I'm always respectful of that. But I'm never going to compromise.
— Spike Jonze

Sci-fi nerds are respectful, honorable. You can trust them.
— Claudia Christian

Sensitive

Beauty of whatever kind, in its supreme development, invariably excites the sensitive soul to tears.
— Edgar Allan Poe

My biggest weakness is my sensitivity. I am too sensitive a person.
— Mike Tyson

Unassuming

I believe that a simple and unassuming manner of life is best for everyone, best both for the body and the mind.
— Albert Einstein

The unassuming youth seeking instruction with humility gains good fortune.
— Joseph Addison

Industrious

Ceaseless
(see page 71)

The only business of the head in the world is to bow a ceaseless obeisance to the heart.
— William Butler Yeats

Time in its irresistible and ceaseless flow carries along on its flood all created things and drowns them in the depths of obscurity.
— Anna Comnena

Diligent

Diligent as one must be in learning, one must be as diligent in forgetting; otherwise the process is one of pedantry, not culture.
— Albert J. Nock

To be idle is a short road to death and to be diligent is a way of life; foolish people are idle, wise people are diligent.
— Buddha

Dynamic
(see page 147)

Physical fitness is not only one of the most important keys to a healthy body, it is the basis of dynamic and creative intellectual activity.
— John F. Kennedy

Instead of this absurd division into sexes they ought to class people as static and dynamic.
— Evelyn Waugh

Hardworking

I'm a typical Capricorn. I'm hardworking, loyal, sometimes stubborn, and I don't believe in astrology.
— Jonah Peretti

I like Cinderella, I really do. She has a good work ethic. I appreciate a good, hard-working gal. And she likes shoes.
— Amy Adams

To build may have to be the slow
and laborious task of years. To
destroy can be the thoughtless act
of a single day.
— Winston Churchill

Poetry is a beautiful way of spoiling
prose, and the laborious art of exchang-
ing plain sense for harmony.
— Horace Walpole

Laborious

When you have people catering to
you non-stop, you lose it. You need
someone to kick you in the butt
every now and then!
— Alexa Vega

It's a non-stop invention, this game
of life, and as soon as you think
you've got it, you lose it.
— Tim Finn

Nonstop

All labor that uplifts humanity
has dignity and importance and
should be undertaken with painstaking excellence.
— Martin Luther King, Jr.

A friend of mine jokes that I have
a painstaking royalty complex.
Like maybe I was a duke in a
past life.
— Frank Ocean

Painstaking

Productive

Should you find yourself in a chronically leaking boat, energy devoted to changing vessels is likely to be more productive than energy devoted to patching leaks.
— Warren Buffett

Everyday, all day I have to be productive. And when I ain't productive, I get concerned.
— Young Jeezy

Purposeful (see page 399)

The idea that everything is purposeful really changes the way you live. To think that everything that you do has a ripple effect, that every action that you make affects other people.
— Victoria Moran

Every person has a longing to be significant; to make a contribution; to be a part of something noble and purposeful.
— John C. Maxwell

Steady

Nothing contributes so much to tranquilize the mind as a steady purpose - a point on which the soul may fix its intellectual eye.
— Mary Wollstonecraft Shelley

Neither the sun nor death can be looked at with a steady eye.
— Francois de La Rochefoucauld

Innovative

Capable
(see page 57)

If we did all the things we are capable of, we would literally astound ourselves.
— Thomas A. Edison

You are capable of more than you know.
— E. O. Wilson

Creative
(see page 131)

A creative man is motivated by the desire to achieve, not by the desire to beat others.
— Ayn Rand

Creativity is allowing yourself to make mistakes. Art is knowing which ones to keep.
— Scott Adams

Dynamic
(see page 147)

Diversity in the world is a basic characteristic of human society, and also the key condition for a lively and dynamic world as we see today.
— Jinato Hu

Imagination is always the fabric of social life and the dynamic of history.
— Simone Weil

Experimental

All progress is experimental.
— John Jay Chapman

You never know with these things when you're trying something new what can happen. This is all experimental.
— Richard Branson

I was obliged to be industrious.
Whoever is equally industrious
will succeed equally well.
— Johann Sebastian Bach

An industrious sinner I much prefer
to a lazy saint.
— Sophie Kerr

Industrious
(see page 293)

It is the mark of a truly intelligent
person to be moved by statistics.
— George Bernard Shaw

I know that I am intelligent,
because I know that I know nothing.
— Socrates

Intelligent
(see page 307)

America is the most inventive country
in the world because everybody has
access to information.
— Tom Clancy

To me, very much of what is artistic
is people's very creative and inventive
ways out of impossible situations.
— James Taylor

Inventive

To expect the unexpected shows a
thoroughly modern intellect.
— Oscar Wilde

In the modern world of business, it
is useless to be a creative, original
thinker unless you can also sell
what you create.
— David Ogilvy

Modern
(see page 339)

Original

Many a man fails as an original thinker simply because his memory it too good.
— Friedrich Nietzsche

Every great architect is - necessarily - a great poet. He must be a great original interpreter of his time, his day, his age.
— Frank Lloyd Wright

Pioneering

Being customer-focused allows you to be more pioneering.
— Jeff Bezos

Rock is all about writing your own script; it's all about pioneering.
— Courtney Love

Innovative and Intelligent

Intelligent

Academic

I look at Google and think they have a strong academic culture. Elegant solutions to complex problems.
— Mark Zuckerberg

The information you get from social media is not a substitute for academic discipline at all.
— Bill Nye

Astute

Marilyn was a great actress, not a dumb blond bombshell. She was very smart, very astute and a good businesswoman.
— Lawrence Schiller

Churchill was the canny political animal, very devious, bursting with energy and determination, learning as hard as he could.
— Lord Mountbatten

Brainy

It's not that I'm so smart, it's just that I stay with problems longer.
— Albert Einstein

It is not enough to have a good mind; the main thing is to use it well.
— Rene Descartes

Bright

Better keep yourself clean and bright; you are the window through which you must see the world
— George Bernard Shaw

Everyone is a genius at least once a year. The real geniuses simply have their bright ideas closer together.
— Georg C. Lichtenberg

Take calculated risks. That is quite
different from being rash.
— George S. Patton

Calculating

I'm pretty calculating. I take stuff
that I know appeals to people's bad
sides and match it up with stuff that
appeals to their good sides.
— Kanye West

The clever cat eats cheese and
breathes down rat holes with
baited breath.
— W. C. Fields

Clever

I am so clever that sometimes I don't
understand a single word of what I
am saying.
— Oscar Wilde

I believe in the compelling power
of love. I do not understand it. I
believe it to be the most fragrant
blossom of all this thorny existence.
— Theodore Dreiser

Cogent

It is in the compelling zest of high
adventure and of victory, and in
creative action, that man finds his
supreme joys.
— Antoine de Saint-Exupery

Coherent

I do insist on making what I hope is sense so there's always a coherent narrative or argument that the reader can follow.
— Howard Nemerov

Work is a way of bringing order to chaos, and there's a basic satisfaction in seeing that we are able to make something a little more coherent by the end of the day.
— Alain de Botton

Cohesive

Most people want to belong to a cohesive, like-minded group.
— Joshua Ferris

I think with world building, it's important to create a sense of culture even if it is just a fantasy, and the best way to do that is to look at a real human culture and see what makes it cohesive.
— Laini Taylor

Coordinated

The world is not to be put in order; the world is order, incarnate. It is for us to harmonize with this order.
— Henry Miller

We now witness the constructive work on a foundation that will endure through the ages. That foundation is the god of science - revealed to us in terms that will harmonize with our intelligence.
— John Fiske

Happiness lies in the joy of achievement and the thrill of creative effort.
— Franklin D. Roosevelt

Creative without strategy is called 'art.' Creative with strategy is called 'advertising.'
— Jef I. Richards

Creative
(see page 131)
(see page 131)

Without deep reflection one knows from daily life that one exists for other people.
— Albert Einstein

I learned never to empty the well of my writing, but always to stop when there was still something there in the deep part of the well, and let it refill at night from the springs that fed it.
— Ernest Hemingway

Deep

The apostolic writings are of three kinds: historical, didactic, and prophetic.
— Philip Schaff

I hope the more didactic approach won't be lost.
— David Attenborough

Didactic

A person who is gifted sees the essential point and leaves the rest as surplus.
— Thomas Carlyle

I know very little about acting. I'm just an incredibly gifted faker.
— Robert Downey, Jr.

Gifted

Innovative
(see page 299)

If you're not failing every now and again, it's a sign you're not doing anything very innovative.
— Woody Allen

Predicting innovation is something of a self-canceling exercise: the most probable innovations are probably the least innovative.
— P. J. O'Rourke

Instructive

Suffering is but another name for the teaching of experience, which is the parent of instruction and the schoolmaster of life.
— Horace

The lecturer should give the audience full reason to believe that all his powers have been exerted for their pleasure and instruction.
— Michael Faraday

Keen

The tongue like a sharp knife...
Kills without drawing blood.
— Buddha

Productivity is never an accident. It is always the result of a commitment to excellence, intelligent planning, and focused effort.
— Paul J. Meyer

Knowledge

Ignorance is the curse of God; knowledge is the wing wherewith we fly to heaven.
— William Shakespeare

To know what you know and what you do not know, that is true knowledge.
— Confucius

Real knowledge is to know the
extent of one's ignorance.
— Confucius

Knowledge is power. Information is
liberating. Education is the prem-
ise of progress, in every society, in
every family.
— Kofi Annan

Knowledgeable

In three words I can sum up
everything I've learned about life:
it goes on.
— Robert Frost

The only person who is educated
is the one who has learned how to
learn and change.
— Carl Rogers

Learned

I am, and ever will be, a white socks,
pocket protector, nerdy engineer.
— Neil Armstrong

I like funny guys and those, for some
reason, tend to be nerdy guys.
— Megan Fox

Nerdy

The Canadian spirit is cautious,
observant and critical where the
American is assertive.
— V. S. Pritchett

On the outskirts of every agony sits
some observant fellow who points.
— Virginia Woolf

Observant

Persuasive

Power is the most persuasive rhetoric.
— Friedrich Schiller

If you can't be persuasive to get
people to believe your crazy idea,
you can just go ahead and build it.
— Jim McKelvey

Philosophical

One of my favorite philosophical tenets
is that people will agree with you only
if they already agree with you. You do
not change people's minds.
— Frank Zappa

A serious and good philosophical
work could be written consisting
entirely of jokes.
— Ludwig Wittgenstein

Profound

I don't need anyone to rectify my
existence. The most profound relationship we will ever have is the one
with ourselves.
— Shirley MacLaine

Buying is a profound pleasure.
— Simone de Beauvoir

Scientific

Our scientific power has outrun our
spiritual power. We have guided mis-
siles and misguided men.
— Martin Luther King, Jr.

We don't devote enough scientific
research to finding a cure for jerks.
— Bill Watterso

If you fight angry, you make a lot
of mistakes, and when you fight a
sharp, witty fighter like me, you
can't make mistakes.
— Floyd Mayweather, Jr.

I wear my Viking helmet because
the horns define how sharp my
brains are. If you try to rub me the
wrong way, I will stick you with
both of my horns.
— Flavor Flav

Sharp

Mr. Obama has an ingenious
approach to job losses: He describes
them as job gains.
— Karl Rove

Let nothing slide, sly remarks.
— Nas

Sly

Wherever smart people work,
doors are unlocked.
— Steve Wozniak

Working hard and working smart
sometimes can be two different things.
— Byron Dorgan

Smart

Fiction and essays can create empathy for the theoretical stranger.
— Barbara Kingsolver

There is no theoretical study of
motherhood. You know, before
I became a mother, I did play a
mother, but I was like - I was more
thinking of my own mother.
— Joan Chen

Theoretical

Thoughtful

A small group of thoughtful people could change the world. Indeed, it's the only thing that ever has.
— Margaret Mead

Great thoughts speak only to the thoughtful mind, but great actions speak to all mankind.
— Theodore Roosevelt

Vivid

Learn from the past, set vivid, detailed goals for the future, and live in the only moment of time over which you have any control: now.
— Denis Waitley

About astrology and palmistry: they are good because they make people vivid and full of possibilities.
— Kurt Vonnegut

Well-informed

My idea of good company is the company of clever, well-informed people who have a great deal of conversation; that is what I call good company.
— Jane Austen

Widespread public access to knowledge, like public education, is one of the pillars of our democracy, a guarantee that we can maintain a well-informed citizenry.
— Scott Turow

Wise

Be happy. It's one way of being wise.
— Sidonie Gabrielle Colette

Wise men speak because they have something to say; Fools because they have to say something.
— Plato

Interesting

Absorbing

Every actor and actress is possessed
of the absorbing passion to create
something distinctive and unique.
— Hattie McDaniel

Generally, my writing is influenced
by living, by absorbing everything
that happens to me and my actions.
— Graham Nash

Addictive

All sins tend to be addictive, and
the terminal point of addiction
is damnation.
— W. H. Auden

Independence is a heady draught,
and if you drink it in your youth,
it can have the same effect on the
brain as young wine does. [...] It is
addictive and with each drink you
want more.
— Maya Angelou

Alluring

Power is not alluring to pure minds.
— Thomas Jefferson

In the education of children there is
nothing like alluring the interest and
affection; otherwise you only make
so many asses laden with books.
— Michel de Montaigne

But humanity also needs dreamers, for whom the disinterested development of an enterprise is so captivating that it becomes impossible for them to devote their care to their own material profit.
— Marie Curie

In general, shorter is better. If you can encapsulate your idea into a single captivating sentence, you're halfway home.
— Len Wein

Captivating

Money doesn't buy elegance. You can take an inexpensive sheath, add a pretty scarf, gray shoes, and a wonderful bag, and it will always be elegant.
— Carolina Herrera

Figure skating is theatrical. It's artistic. It's elegant. It's extremely athletic. And there's a very specific audience for that.
— Johnny Weir

Elegant (see page 155)

It is not easy to be a pioneer - but oh, it is fascinating! I would not trade one moment, even the worst moment, for all the riches in the world.
— Elizabeth Blackwell

The ego is a fascinating monster.
— Alanis Morissette

Fascinating

Hypnotic

There is a very intimate connection between hypnotic phenomena and religion.
— Havelock Ellis

When I play, I very quickly put myself into a light hypnotic trance and compose while playing, drawing directly from the emotions.
— John Fahey

Intriguing

I have always been fascinated by paleontology and prehistoric people, and I've always thought that one of the most intriguing moments in human history was the birth of artistic imagination.
— Kathryn Lasky

I love interacting with different people as I meet them, and I think people are one of God's greatest creations, I really do. They're interesting and intriguing.
— Gladys Knight

Juicy

As social animals, we need to exchange juicy tales about someone - to connect with one another. For millions of years our forebears must have sat around the campfire, whispering about everyone they knew.
— Helen Fisher

If a character dies, you get to do a big, juicy death scene.
— Denis Leary

Listening is a magnetic and strange thing, a creative force. The friends who listen to us are the ones we move toward. When we are listened to, it creates us, makes us unfold and expand.
— Karl A. Menninger

A magnetic personality doesn't necessarily indicate a good heart.
— Laura Linney

Magnetic

I've always chosen incredibly different roles and things that are quite offbeat. That way you're not limited.
— Anna Friel

Some people like neat suburbs. I always am attracted to the rundown and the old and the offbeat.
— William S. Burroughs

Offbeat
(see page 367)

(see page 367)

Good communication is just as stimulating as black coffee, and just as hard to sleep after.
— Anne Morrow Lindbergh

Artists need some kind of stimulating experience a lot of times, which crystallizes when you sing about it or paint it or sculpt it.
— Erykah Badu

Stimulating

Always remember that you are absolutely unique. Just like everyone else.
— Margaret Mead

Human beings, who are almost unique in having the ability to learn from the experience of others, are also remarkable for their apparent disinclination to do so.
— Douglas Adams

Unique
(see page 455)

(see page 455)

Meaningful

Compassionate
(see page 103)

Saving lives is not a top priority in the halls of power. Being compassionate and concerned about human life can cause a man to lose his job.
— Myriam Miedzian

More compassionate mind, more sense of concern for other's well-being, is source of happiness.
— Dalai Lama

Conscious

Life is too short to spend in negativity. So I have made a conscious effort to not be where I don't want to be.
— Hugh Dillon

We should conceive of ourselves not as rulers of Earth, but as highly powerful, conscious stewards: The Earth is given to us in trust, and we can screw it up or make it work well and sustainably.
— Kim Stanley Robinson

Empowering
(see page 185)

I think it's very empowering to be able to have a career and to be a mother. It gives you an amazing sense of self.
— Georgina Chapman

In the network model, rewards come by empowering others, not by climbing over them. If you work in a hierarchy, you may not want to climb to its top.
— John Naisbitt

It is only with the heart that one can
see rightly; what is essential is invisible
to the eye.
— Antoine de Saint-Exupery

Essential

The essential conditions of everything
you do must be choice, love, passion.
— Nadia Boulanger

I believe that you should gravitate to
people who are doing productive and
positive things with their lives.
— Nadia Comaneci

Positive
(see page 389)

Fortune cookies are a good idea. If
the message is positive, it can make
your day a little better.
— Yao Ming

Every person has a longing to be
significant; to make a contribution;
to be a part of something noble
and purposeful.
— John C. Maxwell

Purposeful
(see page 399)

Everything in the universe has a
purpose. Indeed, the invisible intelligence that flows through every
thing in a purposeful fashion is also
flowing through you.
— Wayne Dyer

A life spent making mistakes is not
only more honorable, but more useful than a life spent doing nothing.
— George Bernard Shaw

Useful

Money is the root of all evil, and yet
it is such a useful root that we cannot get on without it any more than
we can without potatoes.
— Louisa May Alcott

Generous - Mysterious

Worthy

The most splendid achievement
of all is the constant striving to
surpass yourself and to be worthy
of your own approval.
— Denis Waitley

You're imperfect, and you're wired
for struggle, but you are worthy of
love and belonging.
— Brene Brown

Mercenary

Abrupt

Revolution, (n.) In politics, an abrupt change in the form of misgovernment.
— Ambrose Bierce

In my work you often get an abrupt shift in time, a jolt. But the emotional logic will take the reader on. I hope. I trust. After all, our memories do not work with any sequential logic.
— Graham Swift

Barbarous

Fashion is something barbarous, for it produces innovation without reason and imitation without benefit.
— George Santayana

The true barbarian is he who thinks everything barbarous but his own tastes and prejudices.
— William Hazlitt

Berserk

When two kids are being completely berserk, and they're naked and throwing food around, sometimes I just let it go because I can see a future where they're going to be dressed, and they're going to be at school.
— Louis C. K.

The behavior of the crowd at Churchill Downs is like 100,000 vicious Hyenas going berserk all at once in a space about the size of a 777 jet or the White House lawn.
— Hunter S. Thompson

One of the truest tests of integrity is its blunt refusal to be compromised.
— Chinua Achebe

Fill your bowl to the brim and it will spill. Keep sharpening your knife and it will blunt.
— Lao Tzu

Blunt

I do not believe in using women in combat, because females are too fierce.
— Margaret Mead

The mountains, the forest, and the sea, render men savage; they develop the fierce, but yet do not destroy the human.
— Victor Hugo

Fierce

A horse never runs so fast as when he has other horses to catch up and outpace.
— Ovid

I'm so fast that last night I turned off the light switch in my hotel room and was in bed before the room was dark.
— Muhammad Ali

Fast
(see page 203)

The foolish and wicked practice of profane cursing and swearing is a vice so mean and low that every person of sense and character detests and despises it.
— George Washington

The secret thoughts of a man run over all things, holy, profane, clean, obscene, grave, and light, without shame or blame.
— Thomas Hobbes

Profane

Rabid

Folks are really tired of this rabid division between Republicans and Democrats. Folks want people to come together and solve the problems and the challenges of America.
— Bev Perdue

A rabid sports fan is one that boos a TV set.
— Jimmy Cannon

Robust

Life is insanely robust, though we can make species go extinct, and this is the bad thing.
— Kim Stanley Robinson

I listen to crazy, robust rock music where they sing their faces off, and soul music, which can be similar.
— Adam Lambert

Rowdy

We're a rock group. we're noisy, rowdy, sensational, and weird.
— Angus Young

The garden is a living, pulsing, singing, scratching, warring, erotic, and generally rowdy thing.
— Diane Ackerman

Savage

Music has charms to sooth a savage breast, to soften rocks, or bend a knotted oak.
— William Congreve

The young man who has not wept is a savage, and the older man who will not laugh is a fool.
— George Santayana

There was a point where I got a
little surly. There were only so many
chicken wings I could serve before
losing the smile on my face.
— Melissa Rauch

And people are intrigued if I really
am as grumpy in real life. People
feel a bit let down if I'm laughing
or smiling.
— Jack Dee

Surly

It's true I don't tolerate fools, but
then they don't tolerate me, so I
am spiky.
— Maggie Smith

Some people were offended by a
show about cougars.
— Courteney Cox

Spiky

People say I am ruthless. I am not
ruthless. And if I find the man
who is calling me ruthless, I shall
destroy him.
— Robert Kennedy

As long as man continues to be the
ruthless destroyer of lower living
beings he will never know health or
peace. For as long as men massacre
animals, they will kill each other.
— Pythagoras

Ruthless

Mercenary and Modern

Modern

Current

All history is current.
— Alice Walker

To me, the real 'state of the union'
is found in how Americans react to
current events.
— Henry Rollins

Fresh

New information makes new and
fresh ideas possible.
— Zig Ziglar

People should think things out fresh
and not just accept conventional
terms and the conventional way of
doing things.
— R. Buckminster Fuller

Innovative (see page 299)

If you're not failing every now and
again, it's a sign you're not doing
anything very innovative.
— Woody Allen

You can't - you can't put a wall up
around here. We tried that in the
'30s. It didn't work.
— Jack Welch

New

With the new day comes new
strength and new thoughts.
— Eleanor Roosevelt

The sun is new each day.
— Heraclitus

We may have all come on different
ships, but we're in the same boat now.
— Martin Luther King, Jr.

Learn from the past, set vivid,
detailed goals for the future, and
live in the only moment of time over
which you have any control: now.
— Denis Waitley

Now

Do not dwell in the past, do not
dream of the future, concentrate
the mind on the present moment.
— Buddha

Confine yourself to the present.
— Marcus Aurelius

Present

By prevailing over all obstacles
and distractions, one may unfail-
ingly arrive at his chosen goal or
destination.
— Christopher Columbus

Excellence is not an exception, it
is a prevailing attitude.
— Colin Powell

Prevailing

A squirrel dying in front of your
house may be more relevant to your
interests right now than people
dying in Africa.
— Mark Zuckerberg

One must be frank to be relevant.
— Corazon Aquino

Relevant

Generous - Mysterious

Youthful
(see page 475)

Being young isn't about age, it's about being a free spirit.
— Twiggy

A youthful mind is seldom totally free from ambition.
— Frances Burney

Mysterious

Ambiguous

I look for ambiguity when I'm writing because life is ambiguous.
— Keith Richards

I would like to provoke ambiguous responses in my readers.
— James Ellroy

Cryptic

The books that help you most are those which make you think that most.
— Pablo Neruda

Way down deep, we're all motivated by the same urges. Cats have the courage to live by them.
— Jim Davis

Dangerous

The true man wants two things: danger and play. For that reason he wants woman, as the most dangerous plaything.
— Friedrich Nietzsche

The fishermen know that the sea is dangerous and the storm terrible, but they have never found these dangers sufficient reason for remaining ashore.
— Vincent Van Gogh

Dark

Deep into that darkness peering, long I stood there, wondering, fearing, doubting, dreaming dreams no mortal ever dared to dream before.
— Edgar Allan Poe

Knowing your own darkness is the best method for dealing with the darknesses of other people.
— Carl Jung

Truth is mysterious, elusive, always
to be conquered.
— Albert Camus

Everything in life is elusive.
— Gloria Vanderbilt

Elusive

Moonlight floods the whole sky
from horizon to horizon; How
much it can fill your room depends
on its windows.
— Rumi

The further in you go, the bigger
it gets.
— John Crowley

Esoteric

On the other hand, what I like my
music to do to me is awaken the
ghosts inside of me. Not the demons,
you understand, but the ghosts.
— David Bowie

Of all ghosts the ghosts of our old
loves are the worst.
— Arthur Conan Doyle

Macabre

Always mystify, mislead and surprise
the enemy if possible.
— Stonewall Jackson

The average man is not hard to mystify.
— Howard Thurston

Mystifying

Mythic

A myth is a way of making sense in a senseless world. Myths are narrative patterns that give significance to our existence.
— Rollo May

Good action films - not crap, but good action films - are really morality plays. They deal in modern, mythic culture.
— Sylvester Stallone

Nocturnal

All architecture is great architecture after sunset; perhaps architecture is really a nocturnal art, like the art of fireworks.
— Gilbert K. Chesterton

We writers are shy, nocturnal creatures. Push us into the light and the light blinds us.
— John Banville

Occult

There is no greater power than the one others do not believe you possess.
— Luis Marques

I am all that hath been, and is, and shall be; and my veil no mortal has hitherto raised.
— Plutarch

Offbeat
(see page 367)

Some people like neat suburbs. I always am attracted to the rundown and the old and the offbeat.
— William S. Burroughs

I think trying to be offbeat is the most boring thing possible.
— Beck

Three may keep a secret, if two of
them are dead.
— Benjamin Franklin

A picture is a secret about a secret,
the more it tells you the less you know.
— Diane Arbus

Secretive

The supernatural is the natural not
yet understood.
— Elbert Hubbard

The word diva to me means doing
something supernatural with something natural.
— Patti LuPone

Supernatural

We know this world intimately and
that is its uncanniness. We cannot
bear our knowledge.
— David Mura

Das Unheimliche - The opposite of
what is familiar.
— German translation

Uncanny

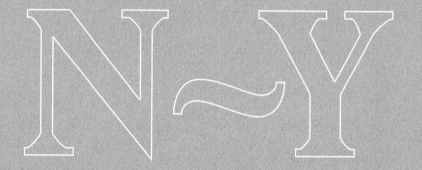

Natural · Youthful

Natural

Earthly

Earthly wisdom is doing what
comes naturally.
— Charles Stanley

I kiss the soil as if I placed a kiss on
the hands of a mother, for the home-
land is our earthly mother.
— Pope John Paul II

Genuine

Genuine poetry can communicate
before it is understood.
— T. S. Eliot

Be still when you have nothing to
say; when genuine passion moves
you, say what you've got to say,
and say it hot.
— D. H. Lawrence

Native

The accent of a man's native country remains in his mind and his
heart, as it does in his speech.
— Francois de La Rochefoucauld

In a funny way, nothing makes you
feel more like a native of your own
country than to live where nearly
everyone is not.
— Bill Bryson

Organic

Organic buildings are the strength
and lightness of the spiders' spin-
ning, buildings qualified by light,
bred by native character to environment, married to the ground.
— Frank Lloyd Wright

Reason is mechanical, wit chemical,
and genius organic spirit.
— Karl Wilhelm Friedrich Schlegel

Only the pure in heart can make
a good soup.
— Ludwig van Beethoven

Power is not alluring to pure minds.
— Thomas Jefferson

Pure

Desperation is the raw material of
drastic change.
— William S. Burroughs

We're always attracted to the edges
of what we are, out by the edges
where it's a little raw and nervy.
— E. L. Doctorow

Raw

When nature exceeds culture, we
have the rustic.
— Confucius

I've always loved the rustic, slightly
worn style of Canvas and that element of an artisanal hand. It's
so inherently chic.
— Jason Wu

Rustic

You can't build a great building on
a weak foundation. You must have
a solid foundation if you're going to
have a strong superstructure.
— Gordon B. Hinckley

I believe in the gold standard.
I like solid lumps of things. You
can always melt them down.
— Suzy Parker

Solid

Natural - Youthful

Textured

The past becomes a texture, an
ambience to our present.
— Paul Scott

Little moments can have a feeling
and a texture that is very real.
— Ralph Fiennes

Unmixed

I wish that every human life might
be pure transparent freedom.
— Simone de Beauvoir

I am too pure for you or anyone.
— Sylvia Plath

Unprocessed

Genius unrefined resembles a
flash of lightning, but wisdom is
like the sun.
— Franz Grillparzer

Some days I would go without
any fire at all, and eat raw frozen
meat and melt snow in my mouth
for water.
— Buffalo Bill

Wild

I don't like formal gardens. I like
wild nature.
— Walt Disney

You can be very wild and still be
very wise.
— Yoko Ono

Naughty

Bawdy

I like bawdy humor. I love bawdy humor, but not dirty humor.
— Betty White

If bawdy talk offend you, we'll have very little of it.
— Shakespeare

Devilish

I like devilish, thorny, dirty, mean roles, muck and mire, unbelievably sad, unbelievably happy, burdened. Inner conflict - that's where drama is.
— Amanda Plummer

This wisdom descendeth not from above, but is earthly, sensual, devilish.
— Bible

Dirty

A dirty joke is a sort of mental rebellion.
— George Orwell

I thank God I was raised Catholic, so sex will always be dirty.
— John Waters

Filthy

I just love getting dirty.
— Robin Wright

I can't do the same thing every night, the same gestures... it's like putting on dirty panties every day.
— Brigitte Bardot

The illicit has an added charm.
— Publius Cornelius Tacitus

If it's illegal to rock and roll, throw
my ass in jail!
— Kurt Cobain

Illicit

Elvis was, at least the times I was
around him, Elvis was a practical
joker. He was always, had some
little mischievous something going.
— Jackie DeShannon

I'm mischievous, but I'm calculated.
— Drake

Mischievous

I'll do shoes for the lady who lunches,
but it would be, like, a really nasty
lunch, talking about men.
— Christian Louboutin

I still got the nasty in me.
— Christina Aguilera

Nasty

To have once been a criminal is no
disgrace. To remain a criminal is
the disgrace.
— Malcolm X

Every society gets the kind of criminal it deserves.
— Robert Kennedy

Nefarious

Playful

It is requisite for the relaxation of the mind that we make use, from time to time, of playful deeds and jokes.
— Thomas Aquinas

The creation of something new is not accomplished by the intellect but by the play instinct acting from inner necessity. The creative mind plays with the objects it loves.
— Carl Jung

Rakish

I would like to be taller, thinner and more rakish looking.
— Michael Sheen

To what a bad choice is many a worthy woman betrayed, by that false and inconsiderate notion, that a reformed rake makes the best husband!
— Samuel Richardson

Raunchy

My mom always taught me to be sweet and polite and cross my legs because it's what the guys like. Actually, they like a raunchy girl once in a while.
— Tiffani Amber Thiessen

The raunchier the better.
— Gene Hackman

Sassy

I've heard I get real sassy onstage, which I'm not in real life! It's fun to be that person for an hour a night.
— Lorde

My personality is up and down, sassy and cheeky.
— Katy Perry

I get really saucy after a few drinks.
Sexy rude, not obnoxious rude.
— Katie Price

I like being saucy, but I'm 73 and a
half. I'm still trying to find my way
between matronly and coltishness.
— Jane Fonda

Saucy

Sex is not sinful, but sin has per-
verted it.
— Walter Lang

Every saint has a past. Every sinner
has a future.
— Oscar Wilde

Sinful

I'm not trashy unless I drink too much.
— Snooki

Keep it classy, bitch.
— Anonymous

Trashy

I'm a good girl because I really believe
in love, integrity, and respect. I'm a bad
girl because I like to tease.
— Katy Perry

Listen, you only tease the ones you love.
— John Boehner

Teasing

As long as war is regarded as wicked,
it will always have its fascination.
— Oscar Wilde

Let's be naughty and save Santa
the trip.
— Gary Allan

Wicked

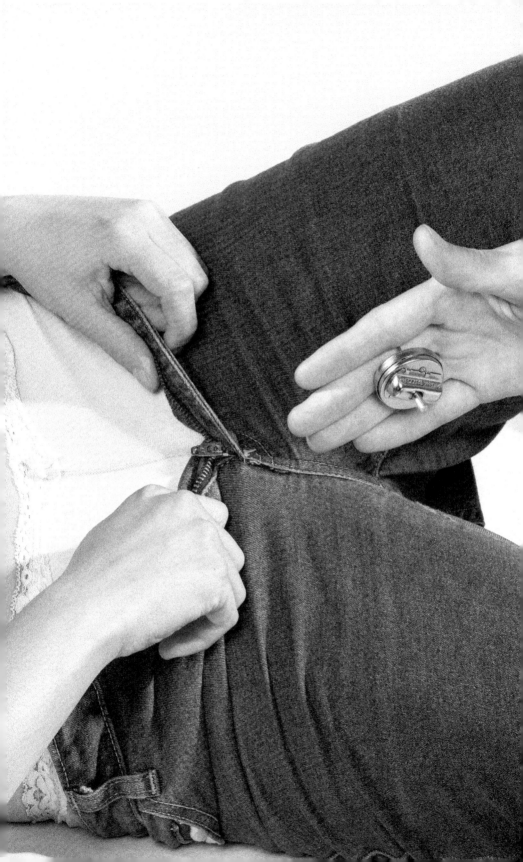

Offbeat

Abnormal

I have a problem when people say
something's real or not real, or normal or abnormal. The meaning of
those words for me is very personal
and subjective.
— Tim Burton

The world is a very abnormal place.
— Salman Rushdie

Abstracted

There is no abstract art. You
must always start with something.
Afterward you can remove all
traces of reality.
— Pablo Picasso

Abstract art will have been good
for one thing: to restore its exact
virginity to figurative art.
— Salvador Dali

Ad Hoc

I have a rather ad hoc and expedient
attitude to structure, particularly as
a design element, and I usually man-
age to prevent it from intruding in
the architectural solution.
— James Stirling

If I didn't know better, I would think
that you were just making definitions
up in an ad hoc manner to avoid
coming to a conclusion which contra-
dicted your prior wishes.
— Greg Erwin

Bizarre

My lifestyle is bizarre, but the only
thing you need to know is where the
darkroom is.
— Robert Mapplethorpe

In L.A., you tend to see a lot of
people do very bizarre things. I love
it.
— Natasha Leggero

In order to be irreplaceable one
must always be different.
— Coco Chanel

If you want to run, run a mile. If
you want to experience a different
life, run a marathon.
— Emil Zatopek

Different

Do not fear to be eccentric in opinion, for every opinion now accepted
was once eccentric.
— Bertrand Russell

Be eccentric now. Don't wait for old
age to wear purple.
— Regina Brett

Eccentric

Most gravity has no known origin.
Is it some exotic particle? Nobody
knows. Is dark energy responsible
for expansion of the universe?
Nobody knows.
— Neil deGrasse Tyson

Everyone is so weird in L.A. that if
you're somewhat normal, it's exotic.
— David Spade

Exotic

The future has already arrived. It's
just not evenly distributed yet.
— William Gibson

Like a ribbon of weed I am flung
far every time the door opens.
— Virginia Woolf

Far-Flung

Flamboyant
(see page 209)

I'm a flamboyant type of guy, a
cooler version of Liberace.
— Usher

Anytime you get men in glitter,
it's a flamboyant occasion!
— Johnny Weir

Fuzzy

There is nothing worse than a sharp
image of a fuzzy concept.
— Ansel Adams

Nostalgia is something we think of
as fuzzy.
— Peter Carey

Obscure

Be obscure clearly.
— E. B. White

A constitution should be short and
obscure.
— Napoleon Bonaparte

Peculiar

Truth is more peculiar than fiction.
— Mira Nair

My lyrics are generated by various
peculiar processes.
— Brian Eno

Quirky

Quirky is what a guy would call a
girl he doesn't understand.
— Kat Dennings

I love nerdy, cute, quirky boys who
don't take themselves too seriously.
— Ariana Grande

People think that I must be a very
strange person. This is not correct.
I have the heart of a small boy. It is
in a glass jar on my desk.
— Stephen King

It's strange that they fear death.
— Jim Morrison

Strange

The sound principle of a topsy-
turvy lifestyle in the framework of
an upside-down world order has
stood every test.
— Karl Kraus

Love works in miracles every day:
such as weakening the strong, and
strengthening the weak; making
fools of the wise, and wise men
of fools; favouring the passions,
destroying reason, and in a word,
turning everything topsy-turvy.
— Marguerite De Valois

Topsy-turvy

You're never too old, too wacky, too wild,
to pick up a book and read to a child.
— Dr. Seuss

Usually the wacky people have the
breakthroughs. The 'smart' people don't.
— Burt Rutan

Wacky

When the going gets weird, the
weird turn pro.
— Hunter S. Thompson

I don't pretend to be captain
weird. I just do what I do.
— Johnny Depp

Weird

Natural - Youthful

Wild

A man without ethics is a wild beast
loosed upon this world.
— Albert Camus

This whole world is wild at heart
and weird on top.
— David Lynch

Optimistic

Confident
(see page 109)

There are times when a leader must move out ahead of the flock, go off in a new direction, confident that he is leading his people the right way.
— Nelson Mandela

Anyone can be confident with a full head of hair. But a confident bald man - there's your diamond in the rough.
— Larry David

Happy
(see page 243)

The purpose of our lives is to be happy.
— Dalai Lama

Whoever is happy will make others happy too.
— Anne Frank

Hopeful

Every heart that has beat strongly and cheerfully has left a hopeful impulse behind it in the world, and bettered the tradition of mankind.
— Robert Louis Stevenson

People want to feel hopeful.
— Michelle Obama

Positive
(see page 389)

It takes but one positive thought when given a chance to survive and thrive to overpower an entire army of negative thoughts.
— Robert H. Schuller

The way positive reinforcement is carried out is more important than the amount.
— B. F. Skinner

Longing is like the rosy dawn.
— Ramakrishna

Inspite of everything, I still believe
people are really good at heart.
— Anne Frank

Rosy

A cloudy day is no match for a
sunny disposition.
— William Arthur Ward

A stale article, if you dip it in a
good, warm, sunny smile, will go off
better than a fresh one that you've
scowled upon.
— Nathaniel Hawthorne

Sunny

I like light, color, luminosity. I like
things full of color and vibrant.
— Oscar de la Renta

I came into music because I thought
the presentation of poetry wasn't
vibrant enough. So I merged improvised poetry with basic rock chords.
— Patti Smith

**Vibrant
(see page 467)**

Natural - Youthful

Passionate

Ambitious

I'm tough, ambitious, and I know
exactly what I want.
— Madonna

I am overly ambitious, because I
realize it can be done.
— Pharrell Williams

Ardent

Self-will so ardent and active that
it will break a world to pieces to
make a stool to sit on.
— Richard Cecil

The ardent golfer would play
Mount Everest if somebody put
a flagstick on top.
— Pete Dye

Aspiring

The barriers are not erected which
can say to aspiring talents and
industry, 'Thus far and no farther.'
— Ludwig van Beethoven

When you are aspiring to the highest place, it is honorable to reach
the second or even the third rank.
— Marcus Tullius Cicero

Bold

Freedom lies in being bold.
— Robert Frost

The bold enterprises are the successful ones. Take counsel of
hopes rather than of fears to win
in this business.
— Rutherford B. Hayes

If you're bored with life - you don't
get up every morning with a burning desire to do things - you don't
have enough goals.
— Lou Holtz

To keep a lamp burning, we have to
keep putting oil in it.
— Mother Teresa

Burning

A small body of determined spirits
fired by an unquenchable faith in
their mission can alter the course
of history.
— Mahatma Gandhi

A determined soul will do more
with a rusty monkey wrench than a
loafer will accomplish with all the
tools in a machine shop.
— Robert Hughes

Determined

To succeed in your mission, you
must have single-minded devotion
to your goal.
— A. P. J. Abdul Kalam

True strength lies in submission
which permits one to dedicate his
life, through devotion, to something
beyond himself.
— Henry Miller

Devoted

Women are strong now. Women are
dominating the charts, and women
are doing it for themselves. We're
kicking butt and taking no prisoners.
— Patti LaBelle

I am dominated by one thing, an irresistible, burning attraction towards
the abstract.
— Gustave Moreau

Domineering

Natural - Youthful

Eager

When a man's willing and eager
the god's join in.
— Aeschylus

The stalwart soul has the will to live
and is eager for the race.
— Taylor Caldwell

Emotional
(see page 179)

People don't buy for logical reasons.
They buy for emotional reasons.
— Zig Ziglar

The computer can't tell you the
emotional story. It can give you
the exact mathematical design, but
what's missing is the eyebrows.
— Frank Zappa

Fiery

Never let go of that fiery sadness
called desire.
— Patti Smith

We can only win by giving everything and being ready to defeat the
adversary with fiery aggression.
— Jurgen Klinsmann

Foolish

If you want to improve, be content
to be thought foolish and stupid.
— Epictetus

Stay hungry, stay foolish.
— Steve Jobs

Furious

I believe any success in life is made
by going into an area with a blind,
furious optimism.
— Sylvester Stallone

I am furious about everything.
— Joan Rivers

Conceptual relativism is a heady
and exotic doctrine, or would be if
we could make good sense of it.
— Donald Davidson

It was heady stuff, recognizing ourselves as an oppressed class, but the
level of discussion was poor.
— Jane O'Reilly

Heady

Your work is to discover your world
and then with all your heart give
yourself to it.
— Buddha

I am interested in personal stories
because that's when people become
expressive, spontaneous and heartfelt.
— Anna Deavere Smith

Heartfelt

For me life is continuously being
hungry. The meaning of life is not
simply to exist, to survive, but to
move ahead, to go up, to achieve,
to conquer.
— Arnold Schwarzenegger

A lion runs the fastest when he
is hungry.
— Salman Khan

Hungry

Great speech is impassioned, small
speech cantankerous.
— Zhuangzi

Impassioned lovers wrestle as one,
lonely man cries for love and has none.
— The Moody Blues

Impassioned

Impulsive

It's very important that young artists push boundaries, because sometimes you have this urge to do something - like the impulsive and dangerous urges I had as a child - and if you don't follow through with it you might miss out on a developmental experience.
— Marina Abramovic

Van Gogh was impulsive.
— Joni Mitchell

Impromptu

Life is a series of natural and spontaneous changes. Don't resist them - that only creates sorrow. Let reality be reality. Let things flow naturally forward in whatever way they like.
— Lao Tzu

Once we believe in ourselves, we can risk curiosity, wonder, spontaneous delight, or any experience that reveals the human spirit.
— E. E. Cummings

Indulgent

Too much of a good thing can be wonderful!
— Mae West

Anything worth doing is worth overdoing.
— Mick Jagger

Intense

The most intense conflicts, if overcome, leave behind a sense of security and calm that is not easily disturbed.
— Carl Jung

Drama usually has some sort of intense conflict.
— Clint Eastwood

In my mind's eye, I visualize how a
particular... sight and feeling will
appear on a print. If it excites me,
there is a good chance it will make
a good photograph.
— Ansel Adams

The highest levels of performance
come to people who are centered,
intuitive, creative, and reflective -
people who know to see a problem
as an opportunity.
— Deepak Chopra

Intuitive

People just don't understand how
obsessed I am with winning.
— Kobe Bryant

To have long term success as a
coach or in any position of leadership, you have to be obsessed in
some way.
— Pat Riley

Obsessed

People misinterpret what I say all
the time: They think I'm being offen-
sive, when really, I'm only being
opinionated.
— Taylor Momsen

I really am opinionated, but not
for long.
— Jerry Lewis

Opinionated

Bathtubs, pools, water - to me, it's a
very essential part of being grounded
and sensual and feeling yourself.
— Andre Balazs

Sensual excess drives out pity in man.
— Marquis de Sade

Sensual

Natural - Youthful

Stirring

It is easier to lead men to combat,
stirring up their passion, than
to restrain them and direct them
toward the patient labors of peace.
— Andre Gide

Just keep stirring the pot, you never
know what will come up.
— Lee Atwater

Strong
(see page 449)

It is easier to build strong children
than to repair broken men.
— Frederick Douglass

Shallow men believe in luck. Strong
men believe in cause and effect.
— Ralph Waldo Emerson

Zealous

A zealous sense of a mission is
only possible when there is oppo-
sition to it.
— D.W. Ewing

People are zealous for a cause
when they are not quite positive
that it is true.
— Bertrand Russell

Positive

Confident
(see page 109)

There are times when a leader must move out ahead of the flock, go off in a new direction, confident that he is leading his people the right way.
— Nelson Mandela

No matter what a woman looks like, if she's confident, she's sexy.
— Paris Hilton

Constructive

I've studied all my musical life, but learning is only good if you do something constructive with it.
— Tony Williams

I love to utilize my celebrity status in a responsible and constructive and substantive manner. I like to get my hands dirty rather than a photo op.
— William Baldwin

Empowering
(see page 185)

Well, I like empowering my clients.
— Gloria Allred

Fame is empowering.
— Charlie Sheen

Let us be grateful to people who make us happy, they are the charming gardeners who make our souls blossom.
— Marcel Proust

Most folks are as happy as they make up their minds to be.
— Abraham Lincoln

Optimism is the faith that leads to
achievement. Nothing can be done
without hope and confidence.
— Helen Keller

Pessimism leads to weakness,
optimism to power.
— William James

Optimistic
(see page 375)

I came into music because I thought
the presentation of poetry wasn't
vibrant enough. So I merged improvised poetry with basic rock chords.
— Patti Smith

I like light, color, luminosity. I like
things full of color and vibrant.
— Oscar de la Renta
Being the richest man in the cem-

Vibrant
(see page 467)

etery doesn't matter to me. Going
to bed at night saying we've done
something wonderful, that's what
matters to me.
— Steve Jobs

Do something wonderful, people
may imitate it.
— Albert Schweitzer

Wonderful

Natural - Youthful

Practical

Befitting

When a friend is in trouble, don't annoy him by asking if there is anything you can do. Think up something appropriate and do it.
— E. W. Howe

Because of the diverse conditions of humans, it happens that some acts are virtuous to some people, as appropriate and suitable to them, while the same acts are immoral for others, as inappropriate to them.
— Thomas Aquinas

Efficient

The higher your energy level, the more efficient your body The more efficient your body, the better you feel and the more you will use your talent to produce outstanding results.
— Tony Robbins

Good writers are those who keep the language efficient. That is to say, keep it accurate, keep it clear.
— Ezra Pound

Functional

Who ever said that pleasure wasn't functional?
— Charles Eames

Design must be functional, and functionality must be translated into visual aesthetics without any reliance on gimmicks that have to be explained.
— Ferdinand Porsche

A good farmer is nothing more nor
less than a handyman with a sense
of humus.
— E. B. White

When you're riding in a time
machine way far into the future,
don't stick your elbow out the window, or it'll turn into a fossil.
— Deep Thoughts by Jack Handy

Handy

If the human race wishes to have
a prolonged and indefinite period
of material prosperity, they have
only got to behave in a peaceful and
helpful way toward one another.
— Winston Churchill

Refusing to ask for help when you
need it is refusing someone the
chance to be helpful.
— Ric Ocasek

Helpful

A people's relationship to their heritage is the same as the relationship
of a child to its mother.
— John Henrik Clarke

It is not the honor that you take
with you, but the heritage you
leave behind.
— Branch Rickey

Heritage
(see page 253)

Dream in a pragmatic way.
— Aldous Huxley

Bill Clinton is a classic, old-school
Southern pragmatic Democrat.
— Monica Crowley

Pragmatic

Realistic

I always like to look on the optimistic side of life, but I am realistic enough to know that life is a complex matter.
— Walt Disney

I'm very realistic. I know my boundaries - I know what I'm good at and what I'm not good at.
— Victoria Beckham

Solid

Rarely do we find men who willingly engage in hard, solid thinking.
— Martin Luther King, Jr.

Be more dedicated to making solid achievements than in running after swift but synthetic happiness.
— A. P. J. Abdul Kalam

Systematic

Science is the systematic classification of experience.
— George Henry Lewes

The founding fathers were not only brilliant, they were system builders and systematic thinkers. They came up with comprehensive plans and visions.
— Ron Chernow

Universal

Today, more than ever before, life must be characterized by a sense of universal responsibility, not only nation to nation and human to human, but also human to other forms of life.
— Dalai Lama

A warm smile is the universal language of kindness.
— William Arthur Ward

The important thing is that men
should have a purpose in life. It
should be something useful, something good.
— Dalai Lama

Have nothing in your house that
you do not know to be useful, or
believe to be beautiful.
— William Morris

Useful

To be a utilitarian means that you
judge actions as right or wrong in
accordance with whether they have
good consequences. So you try to
do what will have the best consequences for all of those affected.
— Peter Singer

Universities are the cathedrals of
the modern age. They shouldn't
have to justify their existence by
utilitarian criteria.
— David Lodge

Utilitarian

Purposeful

Capable
(see page 57)

The difference between what we do and what we are capable of doing would suffice to solve most of the world's problems.
— Mahatma Gandhi

Self-esteem is made up primarily of two things: feeling lovable and feeling capable.
— Jack Canfield

Confident
(see page 109)

Anyone can be confident with a full head of hair. But a confident bald man - there's your diamond in the rough.
— Larry David

Confident people have a way of carrying themselves that makes others more attracted to them.
— Sofia Vergara

Deliberate

The truest wisdom is a resolute determination.
— Napoleon Bonaparte

I am deliberate and afraid of nothing.
— Audre Lorde

Industrious
(see page 293)

I was obliged to be industrious. Whoever is equally industrious will succeed equally well.
— Johann Sebastian Bach

An industrious sinner I much prefer to a lazy saint.
— Sophie Kerr

Old friends pass away, new friends appear. It is just like the days. An old day passes, a new day arrives. The important thing is to make it meaningful: a meaningful friend or a meaningful day.
— Dalai Lama

I would rather die a meaningful death than to live a meaningless life.
— Corazon Aquino

Meaningful
(see page 325)

Always turn a negative situation into a positive situation.
— Michael Jordan

You can't make positive choices for the rest of your life without an environment that makes those choices easy, natural, and enjoyable.
— Deepak Chopra

Positive
(see page 389)

To a resolute mind, wishing to do is the first step toward doing.
— Robert Southey

Marching thus at night, a battalion is doubly impressive. The silent monster is full of restrained power; resolute in its onward sweep, impervious to danger, it looks a menacing engine of destruction, steady to its goal, and certain of its mission.
— Patrick MacGill

Resolute

Natural - Youthful

If you don't have solid beliefs you
cannot build a stable life.
— Alfred A. Montapert

Stable
(see page 441)

To have a healthy culture, you have
to have stable health care financing
and stable arts financing and stable
sports financing, and if you don't
have that, your culture becomes a
parking lot.
— Douglas Coupland

Only the weak are cruel. Gentleness can only be expected from
the strong.
— Leo Buscaglia

Strong
(see page 449)

Nothing is so strong as gentleness,
nothing so gentle as real strength.
— Saint Francis de Sales

Rebellious

Dangerous

An idea that is not dangerous is
unworthy of being called an idea at all.
— Oscar Wilde

The fishermen know that the sea
is dangerous and the storm terrible,
but they have never found these
dangers sufficient reason for
remaining ashore.
— Vincent Van Gogh

Defiant

There is no week nor day nor hour
when tyranny may not enter upon
this country, if the people lose their
roughness and spirit of defiance.
— Walt Whitman

Comedy is defiance. It's a snort of
contempt in the face of fear and anx-
iety. And it's the laughter that allows
hope to creep back on the inhale.
— Will Durst

Contradictory

There's nothing more ironic or contradictory than life itself.
— Robert De Niro

It is not possible to live in this age
if you don't have a sense of many
contradictory forces.
— Rem Koolhaas

Controversial

If journalism is good, it is controversial, by its nature.
— Julian Assange

If an individual wants to be a leader
and isn't controversial, that means
he never stood for anything.
— Richard M. Nixon

You can't get unfamous. You can get
infamous but you can't get unfamous.
— Dave Chappelle

I like being infamous. I think it is
safe being a cult.
— Adam Ant

Infamous

If you're quiet, you're not living.
You've got to be noisy and colorful
and lively.
— Mel Brooks

I write in a noisy, distracting world
so the books can be read there.
— Chuck Palahniuk

Noisy

In an expanding universe, time is on
the side of the outcast.
— Quentin Crisp

I never fit in. I am a true alternative.
And I love being the outcast. That's
my role in life, to be an outcast.
— Meat Loaf

Outcast

I know I'm not the greatest singer or
dancer, but that doesn't interest me.
I'm interested in being provocative
and pushing people's buttons.
— Madonna

Darwin wasn't just provocative in
saying that we descend from the
apes - he didn't go far enough. We
are apes in every way, from our
long arms and tailless bodies to our
habits and temperament.
— Frans de Waal

Provocative

Natural - Youthful

Radical

When you are right you cannot be too radical; when you are wrong, you cannot be too conservative.
— Martin Luther King, Jr.

Radical simply means 'Grasping things at the root.'
— Angela Davis

Scandalous

People love scandal; people love drama. They love stripping away the layers to see what's really in there, and they'll do anything - as well as make it up - to get it.
— Julia Roberts

Love and scandal are the best sweeteners of tea.
— Henry Fielding

Shocking

The writer of originality, unless dead, is always shocking, scandalous; novelty disturbs and repels.
— Simone de Beauvoir

If something is shocking without being funny it's hard to justify.
— Seth MacFarlane

Strong
(see page 449)

A woman is like a tea bag - you can't tell how strong she is until you put her in hot water.
— Eleanor Roosevelt

The world breaks everyone, and afterward, some are strong at the broken places.
— Ernest Hemingway

I can't think of a subject that is
taboo for me, unless it's one I simply
don't know anything about.
— Chris Crutcher

I was always intrigued by the idea
of bringing things together that
are considered taboo or risque
and bringing them together with
something of high elegance and
sophistication.
— Dita Von Teese

Taboo

As every parent knows, children
begin life as uninhibited, unabashed
explorers of the unknown.
— Brian Greene

Success is a welcomed gift for the
uninhibited mind.
— Adlin Sinclai

Uninhibited

Reserved

Absorbed

It is a cursed evil to any man to become as absorbed in any subject as I am in mine.
— Charles Darwin

A man is not idle because he is absorbed in thought. There is a visible labor and there is an invisible labor.
— Victor Hugo

Aloof

The key is in remaining just aloof enough from a painting so that you know when to stop.
— Buffy Sainte-Marie

But curb thou the high spirit in thy breast, for gentle ways are best, and keep aloof from sharp contentions.
— Homer

Bashful

The bashful are always aggressive at heart.
— Charles Horton Cooley

Strange to the world, he wore a bashful look, the fields his study, nature was his book.
— Robert Bloomfield

Cagey

That innate cagey ability of that species of the homo genus is what I fear most!
— Adjesiwor

I'm very cagey about making friends, and I rarely do.
— James Herbert

The pursuit, even of the best things,
ought to be calm and tranquil.
— Marcus Tullius Cicero

Be like a duck. Calm on the surface, but always paddling like the
dickens underneath.
— Michael Caine

Calm

When things are steep, remember
to stay levelheaded.
— Horace

There cannot be a crisis next week.
My schedule is already full.
— Henry A. Kissinger

Collected

Always keep your composure. You
can't score from the penalty box;
and to win, you have to score.
— Horace

Every great player has learned the
two Cs: how to concentrate and how
to maintain composure.
— Byron Nelson

Composed

Sober, steadfast and demure.
— John Milton

Truth is a demure lady, much too
ladylike to knock you on your head
and drag you to her cave.
— William F. Buckley, Jr.

Demure

Natural - Youthful

Discreet

Be discreet in all things, and so render it unnecessary to be mysterious.
— Arthur Wellesley

Thy friend has a friend, and thy friend's friend has a friend; be discreet.
— The Talmud

Humble (see page 287)

Let us touch the dying, the poor, the lonely and the unwanted according to the graces we have received and let us not be ashamed or slow to do the humble work.
— Mother Teresa

Self-praise is for losers. Be a winner. Stand for something. Always have class, and be humble.
— John Madden

Obedient

One act of obedience is better than one hundred sermons.
— Dietrich Bonhoeffer

A great work is made out of a combination of obedience and liberty.
— Nadia Boulanger

Obliging

We cannot always oblige; but we can always speak obligingly.
— Voltaire

To oblige persons often costs little and helps much.
— Baltasar Gracian

Every man's memory is his private
literature.
— Aldous Huxley

I have a private life in which I do
not permit interference. It must
be respected.
— Vladimir Putin

Private

Do not underestimate the determination of a quiet man.
— Iain Duncan Smith

All men's miseries derive from not
being able to sit in a quiet room alone.
— Blaise Pascal

Quiet

We must distinguish between
speaking to deceive and being silent
to be reserved.
— Voltaire

Ignorance is bold and knowledge
reserved.
— Thucydides

Reserved

Where words are restrained, the
eyes often talk a great deal.
— Samuel Richardson

One must learn, if one is to see
the beauty in Japan, to like an
extraordinarily restrained and
delicate loveliness.
— Mary Ritter Beard

Restrained

Serene

For the man sound of body and serene of mind there is no such thing as bad weather; every day has its beauty, and storms which whip the blood do but make it pulse more vigorously.
— George Gissing

Remain calm, serene, always in command of yourself. You will then find out how easy it is to get along.
— Paramahansa Yogananda

Shy

The flower that smells the sweetest is shy and lowly.
— William Wordsworth

Don't try to be what you're not. If you're nervous, be nervous. If you're shy, be shy. It's cute.
— Adriana Lima

Soothing

What I dream of is an art of balance, of purity and serenity devoid of troubling or depressing subject matter - a soothing, calming influence on the mind, rather like a good armchair which provides relaxation from physical fatigue.
— Henri Matisse

A pool is water, made available and useful, and is, as such, infinitely soothing to the western eye.
— Joan Didion

Subdued

We look our best in subdued colors,
sophisticated cuts, and a general air
of sleek understatement.
— Jil Sander

Subdue your appetites, my dears, and
you've conquered human nature.
— Charles Dickens

Tranquil

The pursuit, even of the best things,
ought to be calm and tranquil.
— Marcus Tullius Cicero

The more tranquil a man becomes,
the greater is his success, his influence, his power for good. Calm-
ness of mind is one of the beautiful
jewels of wisdom.
— James Allen

Unflappable

I prided myself on being
unflappable even in the most
chaotic of circumstances.
— Norman Schwarzkop

New Yorkers love the fable of their
own imperturbability, to boast
of how unflappable they remain
whether confronted with a rooster
that has gotten loose in the subway
or a prime minister crossing
Lexington Avenue.
— Jim Dwyer and Kevin Flynn

Sexy

Boiling

When the water starts boiling it is foolish to turn off the heat.
— Nelson Mandela

A good love story always keeps the pot boiling.
— James Patterson

Erotic

I'm not trying to be sexy. It's just my way of expressing myself when I move around.
— Elvis Presley

You don't have to be naked to be sexy.
— Nicole Kidman

Flirtatious

I'm just a natural flirt, but I don't see it in a sexual way. A lot of the time I'm like an overexcited puppy.
— Kylie Minogue

Some women flirt more with what they say, and some with what they do.
— Anna Held

Illicit

There is a charm about the forbidden that makes it unspeakably desirable.
— Mark Twain

The more things are forbidden, the more popular they become.
— Samuel Clemens

Naughty (see page 359)

Mozart was a punk, which people seem to forget. He was a naughty, naughty boy.
— Shirley Manson

I'm a naughty sweetheart.
— Jessica Simpson

So there's nothing more provocative
than taking a genre that everybody
who's cool hates - and then making
it cool.
— Lady Gaga

I know I'm not the greatest singer or
dancer, but that doesn't interest me.
I'm interested in being provocative
and pushing people's buttons.
— Madonna

Provocative

Once I had a rose named after me
and I was very flattered. But I was
not pleased to read the description
in the catalogue: "No good in a bed,
but fine up against a wall."
— Eleanor Roosevelt

Good girls go to heaven, bad girls
go everywhere.
— Mae West

Risque

The most seductive thing about art is
the personality of the artist himself.
— Paul Cezanne

Seduction is always more singular
and sublime than sex and it com-
mands the higher price.
— Jean Baudrillard

Seductive

Conductors must give unmistak-
able and suggestive signals to the
orchestra - not choreography to
the audience.
— George Szell

Statistics are like bikinis. What
they reveal is suggestive, but what
they conceal is vital.
— Aaron Levenstein

Suggestive

Natural - Youthful

Uninhibited

I think we are drawn to dogs
because they are the uninhibited we
might be if we weren't certain we
knew better.
— George Bird Evans

Success is a welcomed gift for the
uninhibited mind.
— Adlin Sinclai

Vivacious

If you're quiet, you're not living.
You've got to be noisy and colorful
and lively.
— Mel Brooks

I'm virile, vigorous, and potent!
— G. Gordon Liddy

Simple

Acoustic

At first acoustics attributed to the different sounds only a limited number of characteristic features.
— Roman Jakobson

One of the ideas behind doing this acoustic record is that I didn't want to have to produce it by committee.
— Robyn Hitchcock

Basic

Our most basic common link is that we all inhabit this planet. We all breathe the same air. We all cherish our children's future. And we are all mortal.
— John F. Kennedy

I had to spend countless hours, above and beyond the basic time, to try and perfect the fundamentals.
— Julius Erving

Clean

Simple can be harder than complex: You have to work hard to get your thinking clean to make it simple. But it's worth it in the end because once you get there, you can move mountains.
— Steve Jobs

Better keep yourself clean and bright; you are the window through which you must see the world.
— George Bernard Shaw

Clear
(see page 93)

When your values are clear to you, making decisions becomes easier.
— Roy E. Disney

People with clear, written goals, accomplish far more in a shorter period of time than people without them could ever imagine.
— Brian Tracy

You must live life in its very
elementary forms.
— Werner Herzog

Elementary, my dear Watson.
— Sherlock Holmes

Elementary

The first essentials, of course, is to
know what you want.
— Robert Collier

To me, business isn't about wearing
suits or pleasing stockholders. It's
about being true to yourself, your
ideas and focusing on the essentials.
— Richard Branson

Essential

Most of the fundamental ideas of science are essentially simple, and may,
as a rule, be expressed in a language
comprehensible to everyone.
— Albert Einstein

The more one does and sees and
feels, the more one is able to do, and
the more genuine may be one's appreciation of fundamental things like
home, and love, and understanding
companionship.
— Amelia Earhart

Fundamental

Common sense is genius in homespun.
— Alfred North Whitehead

All gods are homemade, and it is we
who pull their strings, and so, give
them the power to pull ours.
— Aldous Huxley

Homespun

Honest
(see page 267)

Tricks and treachery are the practice of fools, that don't have brains enough to be honest.
— Benjamin Franklin

Let us raise a standard to which the wise and honest can repair; the rest is in the hands of God.
— George Washington

Humble
(see page 287)

We have to humble ourselves and the way you do that is by serving other people.
— Tim Tebow

I am very humble, and I am very gracious and very grateful for everything that happens to me and about me and around me.
— Lil Wayne

Idyllic

There's something really simple and idyllic about living in a house very close to the water.
— Andrea Riseborough

I was always a happy and loving person. Many would say that I was living an idyllic life.
— Susan Polis Schutz

Minimal

I am a minimalist. I like saying the most with the least.
— Bob Newhart

Prose is architecture and the Baroque age is over.
— Ernest Hemingway

We may brave human laws, but we
cannot resist natural ones.
— Jules Verne

Life is a series of natural and spontaneous changes. Don't resist them -
that only creates sorrow. Let reality
be reality. Let things flow naturally
forward in whatever way they like.
— Lao Tzu

Natural
(see page 353)

Good order is the foundation of all
great things.
— Edmund Burke

Never tell people how to do things.
Tell them what to do and they will
surprise you with their ingenuity.
— George S. Patton

Neat

I'm generally a very pragmatic person: that which works, works.
— Linus Torvalds

Dream in a pragmatic way.
— Aldous Huxley

Pragmatic

Mere color, unspoiled by meaning,
and unallied with definite form, can
speak to the soul in a thousand different ways.
— Oscar Wilde

The open road, especially in the
western United States, is still very
pristine, but everything else around
it has changed.
— Edward Ruscha

Pristine

Pure

Pure mathematics is, in its way, the poetry of logical ideas.
— Albert Einstein

Only the pure in heart can make a good soup.
— Ludwig van Beethoven

Quaint

Baltimore is one of the most beautiful towns, really. And trust me, I don't say that about every place. There is just something so quaint, old and beautiful about this place.
— Polly Bergen

I'm one of those old-fashioned homosexuals, not one of the newfangled ones who are born joining parades.
— Nathan Lane

Rational

Rational beliefs bring us closer to getting good results in the real world.
— Albert Ellis

No rational argument will have a rational effect on a man who does not want to adopt a rational attitude.
— Karl Popper

Self-explanatory

The hardest thing to explain is the glaringly evident which everybody had decided not to see.
— Ayn Rand

We have now sunk to a depth at which restatement of the obvious is the first duty of intelligent men.
— George Orwell

Life is really simple, but we insist
on making it complicated.
— Confucius

When the solution is simple, God
is answering.
— Albert Einstein

Simplistic

Nothing more completely baffles
one who is full of trick and duplicity, than straightforward and simple
integrity in another.
— Charles Caleb Colton

Whoever benefits his enemy with
straightforward intention that man's
enemies will soon fold their hands
in devotion.
— Henry Wadsworth Longfellow

Straightforward

Happiness is not a matter of intensity
but of balance, order, rhythm and
harmony.
— Thomas Merton

Simplicity is the ultimate sophistication.
— Leonardo da Vinci

Uncluttered

Be as simple as you can be; you
will be astonished to see how
uncomplicated and happy your
life can become.
— Paramahansa Yogananda

You're alive. Do something. The
directive in life, the moral imperative was so uncomplicated. It could
be expressed in single words, not
complete sentences. It sounded like
this: Look. Listen. Choose. Act.
— Barbara Hall quotes

Uncomplicated

Natural - Youthful

Well-Made

I praise you because I am fearfully
and wonderfully made; your works
are wonderful, I know that full well.
— Psalm 139:14

Every well built house started in the
form of a definite purpose plus a
definite plan.
— Napoleon Hills

Small

Atomic

Keep up the good work, if only for a
while, if only for the twinkling of a
tiny galaxy.
— Wislawa Szymborska

It has long been an axiom of mine
that the little things are infinitely
the most important.
— Arthur Conan Doyle

Dainty

Nothing's so dainty sweet as lovely
melancholy.
— Francis Beaumont

I'm a girly girl. I'm strong, but I'm
very timid. Very dainty.
— Lil' Kim

Delicate

True strength is delicate.
— Louise Berliawsky Nevelson

The sharp thorn often produces
delicate roses.
— Ovid

Humble
(see page 287)

I stand here before you not as a
prophet, but as a humble servant of
you, the people.
— Nelson Mandela

Talent is God given. Be humble.
Fame is man-given. Be grateful.
Conceit is self-given. Be careful.
— John Wooden

I want to get lean and mean, keep
it minimalist.
— John Cale

I like to be lean. If I get too bulky I
can't move well and I like to move.
When I'm not training, I get really
round and soft.
— Channing Tatum

Lean

The firm, the enduring, the simple,
and the modest are near to virtue.
— Confucius

The modest person is usually
admired, if people ever hear of them.
— E. W. Howe

Modest

For me, I think the bigger something is, the more difficult it is to
make it nimble and fleet afoot.
— Cate Blanchett

The social-media landscape changes
incredibly fast, so you have to be
open-minded and nimble to keep up
with it.
— Alexis Ohanian

Nimble

Find though she be but little,
she is fierce.
— Shakespeare

She was petite, small in that way that
made a man want to slay dragons.
— Julia Quinn

Petite

Natural - Youthful

TALENT
SHOW
AUDITIONS
SIGN IN
➤➤➤

Small and Stable

Stable

Absolute

Absolute identity with one's cause is the first and great condition of successful leadership.
— Woodrow Wilson

Truth is absolute, truth is supreme, truth is never disposable in national political life.
— John Howard

Axiomatic

I know of no more encouraging fact than the unquestionable ability of man to elevate his life by conscious endeavor.
— Henry David Thoreau

When you believe in a thing, believe in it all the way, implicitly and unquestionable.
— Walt Disney

Balanced
(see page 37)

Happiness is not a matter of intensity but of balance, order, rhythm and harmony.
— Thomas Merton

The best and safest thing is to keep a balance in your life, acknowledge the great powers around us and in us. If you can do that, and live that way, you are really a wise man.
— Euripides

A categorical imperative would be one which represented an action as objectively necessary in itself, without reference to any other purpose.
— Immanuel Kant

My conscience is informed by reason. It's like Kant's categorical imperative: behave to others as you would wish they behaved to you.
— Ayaan Hirsi Ali

Categorical

My goal is simple. It is a complete understanding of the universe, why it is as it is and why it exists at all.
— Stephen Hawking

Women. They are a complete mystery.
— Stephen Hawking

Complete

Whosoever desires constant success must change his conduct with the times.
— Niccolo Machiavelli

Excellent firms don't believe in excellence - only in constant improvement and constant change.
— Tom Peters

Constant

Without continual growth and progress, such words as improvement, achievement, and success have no meaning.
— Benjamin Franklin

Our greatest weakness lies in giving up. The most certain way to succeed is always to try just one more time.
— Thomas A. Edison

Continual

Natural - Youthful

Continuous

Continuous effort - not strength or intelligence - is the key to unlocking our potential.
— Winston Churchill

Strength and growth come only through continuous effort and struggle.
— Napoleon Hill

Definite

Create a definite plan for carrying out your desire and begin at once, whether you ready or not, to put this plan into action.
— Napoleon Hill

Winners are people with definite purpose in life.
— Denis Waitley

Heritage (see page 253)

A people's relationship to their heritage is the same as the relationship of a child to its mother.
— John Henrik Clarke

It is not the honor that you take with you, but the heritage you leave behind.
— Branch Rickey

Indelible

Character is the indelible mark that determines the only true value of all people and all their work.
— Orison Swett Marden

'Interview' created indelible images of Pop Art that arrived on people's doorsteps every month.
— Richard Phillips

A stone is ingrained with geological
and historical memories.
— Andy Goldsworthy

It is ingrained in all living creatures, first of all, to preserve their
own safety, to guard against what
is harmful, to strive for what is
advantageous.
— Saint Ambrose

Ingrained

To a resolute mind, wishing to do
is the first step toward doing. But
if we do not wish to do a thing it
becomes impossible.
— Robert Southey

It is only through labor and painful effort, by grim energy and
resolute courage, that we move on
to better things.
— Theodore Roosevelt

Resolute

A joke is a very serious thing.
— Winston Churchill

I want to tell any young girl out
there who's a geek, I was a really
serious geek in high school. It works
out. Study harder.
— Sheryl Sandberg

Serious

Be more dedicated to making solid
achievements than in running after
swift but synthetic happiness.
— A. P. J. Abdul Kalam

If you come from a solid family
structure, it doesn't matter what
you go through in your life.
You're going to be okay.
— Alyssa Milano

Solid

Steadfast

Wealth stays with us a little moment
if at all: only our characters are steadfast, not our gold.
— Euripides

Above our life we love a steadfast friend.
— Christopher Marlowe

Steady

Success is steady progress toward
one's personal goals.
— Jim Rohn

It's the steady, quiet, plodding ones
who win in the lifelong race.
— Robert W. Service

Strong
(see page 449)

A man must be big enough to admit
his mistakes, smart enough to profit
from them, and strong enough to
correct them.
— John C. Maxwell

The world breaks everyone, and
afterward, some are strong at the
broken places.
— Ernest Hemingway

Unflappable

I prided myself on being unflappable even in the most chaotic of
circumstances.
— Norman Schwarzkopf

New Yorkers love the fable of their
own imperturbability, to boast
of how unflappable they remain
whether confronted with a rooster
that has gotten loose in the subway
or a prime minister crossing
Lexington Avenue.
— Jim Dwyer and Kevin Flynn

Strong

Big
(see page 49)

Speak softly and carry a big stick;
you will go far.
— Theodore Roosevelt

You have to think anyway, so why
not think big?
— Donald Trump

Brawny

The brawny mix of extraordinary
sights-weather, politics, races, imagination, corruption and athletics.
— Andrew H. Malcolm

As brawny as Chicago.
— Martina Navratilova

Burly

We gain strength, and courage, and
confidence by each experience in
which we really stop to look fear in
the face... we must do that which we
think we cannot.
— Eleanor Roosevelt

When you go through hardships
and decide not to surrender, that
is strength.
— Arnold Schwarzenegger

Capable
(see page 57)

If we did all the things we are
capable of, we would literally
astound ourselves.
— Thomas A. Edison

Self-esteem is made up primarily
of two things: feeling lovable and
feeling capable.
— Jack Canfield

There is a healthful hardiness
about real dignity that never dreads
contact and communion with others
however humble.
— Washington Irving

Peace and plenty breed cowards;
hardness over hardiness is the mother.
— William Shakespeare

Hardy

I also got a real heavy duty blood
clot and internal bleeding from
where I was shot in the stomach
with a beanbag bullet that the
police use for crowd control.
— Johnny Knoxville

Motown will always be a heavy-
duty part of my life because those
are my roots.
— Smokey Robinson

Heavy-Duty

My four years in the Marine Corps
left me with an indelible understanding of the value of leadership skills.
— Frederick W. Smith

Memory is more indelible than ink.
— Anita Loos

Indelible

If you seek truth you will not seek
victory by dishonorable means,
and if you find truth you will
become invincible.
— Epictetus

Whoever is winning at the moment
will always seem to be invincible.
— George Orwell

Invincible

Manly

Go forth to meet the shadowy future without fear and with a manly heart.
— Henry Wadsworth Longfellow

The strong manly ones in life are those who understand the meaning of the word patience.
— Tokugawa Ieyasu

Mighty

From a small seed a mighty trunk may grow.
— Aeschylus

He who conquers others is strong;
He who conquers himself is mighty.
— Lao Tzu

Powerful

Ideas are more powerful than guns.
— Joseph Stalin

The less effort, the faster and more powerful you will be.
— Bruce Lee

Resilient

Man never made any material as resilient as the human spirit.
— Bernard Williams

The Taliban is resilient.
— Leon Panetta

Rugged

I'm raw, I'm rugged and raw! I repeat, if I die. My seed'll be ill like me.
— Ghostface Killah

Honor is like an island, rugged and without shores; once we have left it, we can never return.
— Nicholas Boilea

A house must be built on solid
foundations if it is to last.
— Sai Baba

I want to make a good, solid
kung fu movie.
— Keanu Reeves

Solid

Heap high the board with plenteous
cheer and gather to the feast, And
toast the sturdy Pilgrim band whose
courage never ceased.
— Alice W. Brotherton

A true friend is a sturdy shelter; he
who finds one finds a treasure.
— Unknown

Sturdy

Tough times never last, but tough
people do.
— Robert H. Schuller

Life is tough, but it's tougher when
you're stupid.
— John Wayne

Tough

Unique

Amazing
(see page 23)

I am constantly amazed by Tina Fey.
And I am Tina Fey.
— Tina Fey

It is amazing what you can accomplish if you do not care who gets the credit.
— Harry S. Truman

Authentic

The most authentic thing about us is our capacity to create, to overcome, to endure, to transform, to love and to be greater than our suffering.
— Ben Okri

Without culture, and the relative freedom it implies, society, even when perfect, is but a jungle. This is why any authentic creation is a gift to the future.
— Albert Camus

Confident
(see page 109)

To succeed in life, you need two things: ignorance and confidence.
— Mark Twain

With confidence, you have won before you have started.
— Marcus Garvey

Creative
(see page 131)

True art is characterized by an irresistible urge in the creative artist.
— Albert Einstein

A creative man is motivated by the desire to achieve, not by the desire to beat others.
— Ayn Rand

In order to be irreplaceable one
must always be different.
— Coco Chanel

If a man does not keep pace with his
companions, perhaps it is because he
hears a different drummer. Let him
step to the music which he hears,
however measured or far away.
— Henry David Thoreau

Different

I guess the issue for me is to keep
things dynamic.
— Robert Downey, Jr.

The most dynamic cities have
always been immersed in the critical
innovations of their time.
— Geoff Mulgan

Dynamic
(see page 147)

To create something exceptional,
your mindset must be relentlessly
focused on the smallest detail.
— Giorgio Armani

It is extremely dangerous to encour-
age people to see themselves as
exceptional, whatever the motivation.
— Vladimir Putin

Exceptional

Cinderella is not only an iconic character when it comes to beauty, grace
and fairytale love, but also shoes.
— Christian Louboutin

I think every decade has an iconic
blonde, like Marilyn Monroe or
Princess Diana and, right now,
I'm that icon.
— Paris Hilton

Iconic

Natural - Youthful

Interesting
(see page 319)

The most interesting information comes from children, for they tell all they know and then stop.
— Mark Twain

Contrast is what makes photography interesting.
— Conrad Hall

Offbeat
(see page 367)

Some people like neat suburbs. I always am attracted to the rundown and the old and the offbeat.
— William S. Burroughs

I grew up watching all these crazy movies, European movies and stuff, and I guess that I always laughed at things that were a little more offbeat.
— Louis C. K.

Rebellious
(see page 405)

Sons have always a rebellious wish to be disillusioned by that which charmed their fathers.
— Aldous Huxley

I am extremely rebellious. I have this strong, defiant spirit.
— Yoko Ono

Singular

I think every single person perceives things differently. We are all singular.
— Julia Leigh

When you start a company, it's a singular focus. You have the wind at your back.
— Howard Schultz

Everything that is new or uncommon raises a pleasure in the imagination, because it fills the soul with an agreeable surprise, gratifies its curiosity, and gives it an idea of which it was not before possessed.
— Joseph Addison

When you do the common things in life in an uncommon way, you will command the attention of the world.
— George Washington Carver

Uncommon

A bird without wings and a man without art are both condemned to wander in low places; they can never soar up to those unrivaled heights.
— Mehmet Murat ildan

Autobiography is an unrivaled vehicle for telling the truth about other people.
— Philip Guedalla

Unrivaled

Valuable

Admired

I don't pity any man who does hard
work worth doing. I admire him.
— Theodore Roosevelt

You always admire what you really
don't understand.
— Blaise Pascal

Flawless

An idea can be as flawless as can be,
but its execution will always be full
of mistakes.
— Brent Scowcroft

Success doesn't necessarily come
from breakthrough innovation but
from flawless execution.
— Naveen Jain

Heritage

A people's relationship to their heritage is the same as the relationship
of a child to its mother.
— John Henrik Clarke

It is not the honor that you take
with you, but the heritage you
leave behind.
— Branch Rickey

Precious

When you arise in the morning,
think of what a precious privilege it
is to be alive - to breathe, to think,
to enjoy, to love.
— Marcus Aurelius

My favorite things in life don't cost
any money. It's really clear that the
most precious resource we all have
is time.
— Steve Jobs

We hold our heads high, despite the
price we have paid, because freedom is priceless.
— Lech Walesa

Skating has given me so much that
it's priceless.
— Michelle Kwan

Priceless

There is nothing on this earth more
to be prized than true friendship.
— Thomas Aquinas

Among my most prized possessions
are words that I have never spoken.
— Orson Scott Card

Prized

Rare is the union of beauty and purity.
— Juvenal

All things excellent are as difficult
as they are rare.
— Baruch Spinoza

Rare

I have a private life in which I do
not permit interference. It must
be respected.
— Vladimir Putin

I believe in human beings, and
that all human beings should be
respected as such, regardless of
their color.
— Malcolm X

Respected

Natural - Youthful

Scarce

Capital isn't scarce; vision is.
— Sam Walton

When words are scarce they are
seldom spent in vain.
— William Shakespeare

Special

We are just an advanced breed of
monkeys on a minor planet of a very
average star. But we can understand
the universe. That makes us something very special.
— Stephen Hawking

Please don't call me arrogant, but
I'm European champion and I think
I'm a special one.
— Jose Mourinho

Treasured

Books are the treasured wealth of
the world and the fit inheritance of
generations and nations.
— Henry David Thoreau

'Meet the Press' is the oldest and
most treasured public affairs show
on television.
— David Shuster

Worthwhile

Only a life lived for others is
a life worthwhile.
— Albert Einstein

Success is the progressive realization of predetermined, worthwhile,
personal goals.
— Paul J. Meyer

Vibrant

Alive

Today you are you! That is truer
than true! There is no one alive who
is you-er than you!
— Dr. Seuss

When you arise in the morning,
think of what a precious privilege it
is to be alive - to breathe, to think,
to enjoy, to love.
— Marcus Aurelius

Amazing

When you have confidence, you can
have a lot of fun. And when you have
fun, you can do amazing things.
— Joe Namath

Work hard, be kind, and amazing
things will happen.
— Conan O'Brien

Beautiful
(see page 43)

The best and most beautiful things
in the world cannot be seen or even
touched - they must be felt with
the heart.
— Helen Keller

Never lose an opportunity of seeing anything beautiful, for beauty
is God's handwriting.
— Ralph Waldo Emerson

Bright

If you paint in your mind a picture
of bright and happy expectations,
you put yourself into a condition
conducive to your goal.
— Norman Vincent Peale

When I look into the future, it's so
bright it burns my eyes.
— Oprah Winfrey

A man must live like a great brilliant flame and burn as brightly as he can.
— Boris Yeltsin

Kelly, Kelly, Kelly. I love your voice man, you give me chills... Brilliant.
— Randy Jackson

Brilliant

I guess the issue for me is to keep things dynamic.
— Robert Downey, Jr.

Dynamic activity and deep rest of the mind are complementary to each other.
— Deepak Chopra

Dynamic
(see page 147)

I will only observe, that that ethereal sense - sight, and touch, which is at the other extremity of the scale, have from time acquired a very remarkable additional power.
— Jean Anthelme Brillat-Savarin

Ethereal minstrel pilgrim of the sky!
— Williams Wordsworth

Ethereal
(see page 195)

Pull up in that super-coupe: you know them diamonds glistening. Too much money in the room, guess I hit her in the kitchen then.
— Young Jeezy

Whether whiteness whisks soft shadows away, feel flows, white hot glistening shadowy flows.
— The Beach Boys

Glistening

Natural - Youthful

Glossy

Glossy, efficient prose, garnished
with a pinch of irony and a dab of
melodrama.
— Michiko Kakutani

I love the confidence makeup gives me.
— Tyra Banks

Lively

Life is a lively process of becoming.
— Douglas MacArthur

If you're quiet, you're not living.
You've got to be noisy and colorful
and lively.
— Mel Brooks

Luminous

Painting is by nature a luminous
language.
— Robert Delaunay

The dancer's body is simply the
luminous manifestation of the soul.
— Isadora Duncan

Radiant

The ground we walk on, the plants
and creatures, the clouds above constantly dissolving into new formations
- each gift of nature possessing its
own radiant energy, bound together
by cosmic harmony.
— Ruth Bernhard

Everywhere across whatever sorrows
of which our life is woven, some radiant joy will gaily flash past.
— Nikolai Gogol

To be perfectly, brutally honest,
those of us who are still carrying
diaper everywhere we go are not at
our most scintillating time of life...
— Louise Lague

He holds him with his glittering eye.
— Samuel Taylor Coleridge

Scintillating

Little children love bright, shiny
things – and in my experience, most
grown-up women aren't very different!
— Sheherazade Goldsmith

The shiny red color of the soles has
no function other than to identify to
the public that they are mine.
— Christian Louboutin

Shinny

Mirth is the sweet wine of human
life. It should be offered sparkling
with zestful life unto God.
— Henry Ward Beecher

I love skating and sparkling and fly-
ing around the ice, and people clap
for you. It's an amazing feeling.
— Johnny Weir

Sparkling

Natural - Youthful

EXIT

Vibrant and Youthful

Youthful

Active

I've found that luck is quite predict-able. If you want more luck, take more chances. Be more active. Show up more often.
— Brian Tracy

Fresh activity is the only means of overcoming adversity.
— Johann Wolfgang von Goethe

Current

If you keep yourself alive and current, funny is funny.
— Alan King

The outside world is pretty foreign to me.
— Kurt Cobain

Enthusiastic

Be interesting, be enthusiastic... and don't talk too much.
— Norman Vincent Peale

We're just enthusiastic about what we do.
— Steve Jobs

Fresh

People should think things out fresh and not just accept conventional terms and the conventional way of doing things.
— R. Buckminster Fuller

Tomorrow is always fresh, with no mistakes in it.
— Lucy Maud Montgomery

Telling a story in a futuristic world gives you this freedom to explore things that bother you in contemporary times.
— Suzanne Collins

It always struck me that Africa was, in a strange way, a futuristic place and had elements and vibes and spirits that were going to inform the future.
— Damon Albarn

Futuristic

Life is a lively process of becoming.
— Douglas MacArthur

A lively understandable spirit once entertained you. It will come again. Be still. Wait.
— Theodore Roethke

Lively

To expect the unexpected shows a thoroughly modern intellect.
— Oscar Wilde

Black-and-white always looks modern, whatever that word means.
— Karl Lagerfeld

Modern
(see page 339)

Happiness is not something you postpone for the future; it is something you design for the present.
— Jim Rohn

Confine yourself to the present.
— Marcus Aurelius

Present

Natural - Youthful

Rambunctious

The golden age, when rambunctious spirits were regarded as the source of evil.
— Friedrich Nietzsche

He's very rambunctious. We had a hard time loading him up to get him here. We finally got him to go along.
— Jacob Jones

Relevant

A squirrel dying in front of your house may be more relevant to your interests right now than people dying in Africa.
— Mark Zuckerberg

One must be frank to be relevant.
— Corazon Aquino

Sassy

My personality is up and down, sassy and cheeky.
— Katy Perry

I've heard I get real sassy onstage, which I'm not in real life! It's fun to be that person for an hour a night.
— Lorde

Sprightly

Tossing their heads in sprightly dance.
— William Wordsworth

These flowers, which were splendid and sprightly, waking in the dawn of the morning, in the evening will be a pitiful frivolity, sleeping in the cold night's arms.
— Pedro Calderon de la Barca

Acknowledgments

Verdes would like to thank the talented linguist René Fassbender for figuring out how to put a sea of words into a series of buckets. We would like to thank the wise ways of Michael Ian Kaye. We would like to thank the skillful hands of Young Professionals and the clever mind of Chris Maggio. We would like to thank the First Amendment for all the quotes. We would also like to thank Nicholas Bethlem and Dorothy Smith for the time and tireless labor.

Each year more and more words enter our language. As our lexicon grows, so will volumes of this book. To submit new words for consideration please contact us at:

info@browniesguidetoexpertlydefinedideas.com

CPSIA information can be obtained
at www.ICGtesting.com
Printed in the USA
BVOW11s0222100416

443302BV00013B/15/P